What Childcare owners are saying about Improving The Business of Childcare

Allan's book would have been invaluable to me when I first decided to open a nursery school over eight years ago. However, reading it now as an experienced twice *Outstanding* owner has highlighted how much I have learned about being in this sometimes overwhelming sector!

Allan cleverly describes innovative ways to promote your nursery business and explains how to keep ahead of the competition. This has left me buzzing with ideas for my next marketing campaign.

If you're already in the nursery sector or about to open your own *Early Years* setting, this book is a must-read. Don't forget your *Post-it* notes to mark those *light bulb* insights!

Donna Row
Proprietor, Yorley Barn Nursery School

Allan's book has reminded me that success can be planned for and achieved, and that daily stresses can easily be managed, if time is taken to reflect and act on the needs of my business. As an experienced day nursery owner I have found *Improving the Business of Childcare* to be an invaluable tool that helps my business continuously evolve and stay ahead. Thank you Allan!

Lynne Stanley
Proprietor, Crown Kindergartens Day Nursery

As an experienced nursery owner who has managed and led my setting for over 20 years I can see so much of the old me in these pages alongside glimpses of the current me. It has taken a long time to develop the business side of my *Early Years* setting. This book can fast forward that time-frame for fledgling owners.

For experienced owners this book can awaken your need to not just care about children but to gain financially too. To develop a balance between nurturing a strong pedagogical approach alongside a passion for financial rewards that come from a successful business. It is easy to read with interesting strategies that are simple to apply.

Getting it right for children is often the aim for the *Early Years*. It is now time for us to allow our businesses to grow up as much as we allow our children to learn and grow. As you read Allan's book note where you can make changes. I promise you will find ideas that will make you think. Each section enables you to refine your vision, reflect on your current positioning and enable you to move forward to where you deserve to be.

Debbie Gunn
Proprietor, D-Dee's Day Nursery

Improving the Business of Childcare is concise and easy to read. Each chapter has a clear message with lots of practical tips and real examples from childcare businesses that make it easy to relate to your own business.

Allan Presland has extensive knowledge of running successful businesses and very specific knowledge about our sector. This book will reassure you about what's going well in your childcare business and make you think about areas for improvements, with some great advice on how to drive those improvements.

Jo Morris
Playsteps Day Nursery

Improving the Business of Childcare is an enlightening read, full of intriguing stories and practical business advice for improving your Childcare setting.

Many of the topics covered take me back to when I was first starting out on my childcare business journey, and yet other tips are improvements we haven't implemented into our nurseries but soon will.

At long last the sector has a guide to running a nursery business and I will be giving a copy of Allan's book to each of my nursery managers.

Cheryl Hadland
MD and Proprietor, Hadland Care Group

I've read hundreds of similar business books and I expected to get some interesting information about the childcare sector. What I got was so much more.

I'm a seasoned professional businessman and yet I found Allan providing insights into approaches to business that, whilst he has applied them to the childcare sector, I believe are appropriate for all businesses, whatever their size.

This book is a *must-read* for anyone in the Childcare sector and a *should-read* for any business leader keen to develop their business profitably.

It is a glorious mix of hard-nosed business advice, passion and stories. I recommend it.

Chris Hughes
Vistage Chairman

Improving
The Business
of Childcare

**Empowering Childcare owners
to achieve financial success**

ALLAN PRESLAND

WRITING MATTERS PUBLISHING

IMPROVING THE BUSINESS OF CHILDCARE

Empowering Childcare owners To achieve financial success

Copyright 2017 Allan Presland

First published in 2017

Writing Matters Publishing (UK)
info@writingmatterspublishing.com
www.writingmatterspublishing.com

ISBN 978-0-9956051-4-5

Please Note: *Improving the Business of Childcare* is intended as information only and does not constitute specific financial, investment, taxation or legal advice unique to your situation. It is for educational purposes only. The Author, Publisher and Resellers accept no responsibility for loss, damage or injury to persons or their belongings as a direct or indirect result of reading this book.

Dedication

This book is dedicated to my brother, David Presland, who, in the most incredible act of bravery, on the 7th August 2015, saved my life.

Contents

At a Glance

National Surveys

Improving the Business of Childcare draws on the results of ongoing national surveys of Childcare settings in the UK. A 2016 survey showed that 49% of Childcare settings do not expect to trade profitably.

The independent *Parenta National Childcare Survey (2016)* found similar results.

Profitability

The author, Allan Presland has visited over a thousand childcare providers during his career as MD of the *Parenta Group,* both in the UK and abroad and has consistently found *profitability* to be the single most business related topic of discussion.

Glaring business skills gap

He has noticed that whilst all of them have an inspirational passion for their vocation, many childcare owners inevitably have business skills gaps.

A guide to trading profitably

Allan has therefore written an easy-to-read book for Childcare owners to help them understand these gaps and teach them how to overcome them. The result is an invaluable reference manual to help childcare owners run their businesses more successfully.

Key Business Skills

Improving the Business of Childcare is designed to help Childcare owners to significantly improve their business and to enable them to trade more profitably.

Topics include:

- Vision and Values statements.
- Marketing and Occupancy.
- Identifying and Converting Target Customers.
- Customer Engagement.
- Staff Engagement and Staff Management.
- Pricing and Value-Add Services.
- Collecting Fees.
- Understanding Finance and Financial Reporting.
- Systems and Processes.
- Measuring Success, Metrics and Dashboards.

The key results are maximising occupancy, engaged customers and staff, effective collection of fees, tracking performance and creating a sustainable, profitable business.

Online Resources

The book is supported with online resources via:

www.Parenta.com/resources

The Author

Allan Presland is the founder and CEO of *Parenta,* the UK's largest provider of business support systems for the *Early Years* sector. *Parenta* works with over 5,000 childcare providers of various sizes worldwide.

Allan is also the founder of the *ParentaTrust,* a charity that provides pre-school education to disadvantaged and orphaned children in East Africa.

Introduction

I have been privileged to spend the last couple of decades working with numerous childcare providers. In fact, I have personally visited over a thousand settings, not just in the UK, but also in the USA, Australia and New Zealand, Africa and Europe.

In doing so, I have seen a consistent pattern. Childcare owners who are skilled and passionate about their vocation, who work incredibly hard and yet have businesses that are struggling financially, or not returning the rewards their owners expect.

These business owners have often spent years learning their vocation and eventually saved up enough money to open their own nursery. They may have a huge bank loan or a second mortgage which they have invested in the building. It's been painted and decorated, they've hired the staff and engaged with them, they've built brilliant relationships with the children and their parents, they even gone into battle with their regulatory body and got a good rating, and then … the bills keep piling up, the tax man is on the phone every week and it becomes increasingly difficult to make ends meet. The stress is enormous, and the impact on personal relationships is unbearable.

The problem is that whilst they are vocationally exceptional, as entrepreneurs running small businesses they often have had no formal training in business, management, marketing or accountancy. And why would they? They are *Early Years* experts who have been taught to nurture, not to run a business with all the pressures that can bring.

This is backed up by published data. According to a study by the *National Day Nurseries Association (2016)*, 49% of nurseries in the UK are not forecasting to make a profit this year. In addition, my company, *Parenta*, undertakes a *National Childcare* survey every year and came up with very similar results. In this case, the evidence we uncovered concluded that 40% of nurseries did not expect to make a profit this year. At the same time according to official figures the number of childminders continues to spiral downwards.

The question that intrigued me most was: *Why do half of these highly skilled and passionate child owners and staff struggle to make a profit?*

As I studied this issue, it re-confirmed my initial conclusions: that the actual *care* was rarely the issue. And looking at the data specifically within the *Parenta National Childcare Survey*, it became increasingly clear that the most successful providers were doing something fundamentally different to those who were less successful. The most successful providers consistently return profits, (often very substantial profits), whilst offering an exceptional level of care and education to children and a remarkable experience for the parents.

Critically in an industry renowned for paying poorly, these settings also pay above the norm, sometimes significantly so. And before the argument is made, I have seen this in deprived areas, as well as more affluent areas.

And so *Improving the Business of Childcare* collates the experiences that I have observed working with so many childcare businesses and highlights what the most successful are doing that makes them different - that enables them to be successful and profitable.

Profit is one of those emotive words that often sits uncomfortably with a Care sector. But I make no excuses for talking about the need for childcare providers to become profitable - it is clearly a prerequisite to survival, not only of the individual setting but also for the sector as a whole.

Running any business is exceedingly difficult. Running a Childcare business is harder still. Not only is the business exceedingly complex, but you have to operate under one of the strictest compliance regimes available and deal with an incredibly emotive subject, as well as engaging with the public day in and day out.

The reality is, however, to deliver exceptional quality childcare, you must be making an acceptable profit, not merely break-even. It's the only way to continue to invest in services, in infrastructure, in staff and ultimately, but critically, in offering exceptional support and education for children.

And this includes those who are *not for profit*. *Not for profit* has always struck me as a meaningless term because it doesn't mean what it says. What is meant is *profits are not for shareholder distribution*.

So let's make it clear, for those pre-schools and community run settings, I suggest that you do focus on making a profit so that you can invest in improving your service, your facilities or staff. Again, we'll talk about the critical importance of profitability later on, but for now, it's important to remember that as well as meeting all of your outgoings, being profitable also affects your credit rating and thus your ability to finance the business as needed, not to mention increasing staff pay.

One of the things that has become apparent to me is that less successful *Early Years* businesses don't recognise who the actual customer is. The customer is the parent who pays you, not the child. You are running a business, so customer engagement, or in this case, parent-engagement is a prerequisite, as is exceptional customer retention.

Throughout this book, we will discuss how the most successful childcare providers create engaging, exceptional, customer experiences.

I also explain in practical terms the specific systems, tools and strategies that the most successful nurseries use to ensure they thrive.

Within the *Parenta National Childcare Survey*, the following issues were identified as causing concern amongst providers: dealing with staff, dealing with poor occupancy and strong competition, dealing with cash collection and financial controls and lastly ensuring there is sufficient engagement with parents.

Based on this information, *Improving the Business of Childcare* covers the key business facets of ensuring that the nursery has a clear vision and that its values are understood by all, something that all the successful settings have in place.

- It clearly shows the metrics that should be tracked and explains both why and how.

- It addresses the issue of ensuring that your setting is full by detailing strategies to increase occupancy, and explains the real costs of not having adequate and robust customer conversion strategies in place.

- It provides an overview of financial systems which are understandable by non-financial managers and details why it's essential that fee collection systems are fully automated.

- It explains how to motivate and engage staff, as well as how to measure that engagement.

Lastly, it covers the needs of parents, how to create the optimal customer experience and how to ensure that parents provide the online testimonials so urgently needed for the promotion of the business.

And all of this is backed up with free guides and templates to provide further advice, support and guidance.

Improving the Business of Childcare is then a handbook to improve the profitability of any childcare setting.

It sets out a sequence of must-haves to ensure that the building blocks of a childcare business are robust – freeing you to spend more time looking after children, and minimising the stresses of running the business.

I am passionate about ensuring that Childcare businesses are successful. My own personal vision is:

*'A world in which every child is loved
and fulfills their potential.'*

I'll talk about why that's my vision, and how I translate this through my work at *Parenta*, and through our charity, the *ParentaTrust*, in a subsequent chapter. But for now, let's be very clear up front. Children will never fulfill their potential unless we have a childcare sector that is thriving. You will already be aware of the countless studies that link early year's education with success later in life.

Before we go any further together, though, it's time for a confession. I have never run a nursery. So, you may well ask, how am I qualified to write this book? Well, firstly, I have run numerous successful and profitable businesses. Some have been new-starts, many turnarounds and one corporate. This has given me a unique commercial perspective of what works in business and I've used that knowledge to advise Childcare settings I have visited.

Secondly, as I've mentioned, I have been to at least a thousand childcare settings and have met so many brilliant nursery owners and managers, having been in the sector for nearly two decades. Each one has a unique perspective on what works and what doesn't, and over time it becomes clear that there are distinct patterns. As I've observed those patterns, the drivers of success haves become increasingly apparent.

Combine these two aspects together and you have a book that incorporates the best ideas and methods that I've seen within childcare settings with well-proven and profitable systems, which have been used across many successful non-childcare businesses.

Finally, I've taken the liberty of adding a *rant* at the end of each chapter. *Al's Rant* is my little bit of *kicking off* against those things that I don't like or understand!

Apologies in advance to anyone this offends, but if you can't *kick-off* in your own book, where can you?

I want you to find this book of value, so you can translate these strategies and systems to improve the business side of your childcare setting. Even if your business is already thriving, I hope there are still ideas that will help you grow further. The good news is that the vast majority of my suggestions are free to implement, so even if your setting is struggling, you don't need to invest much to start succeeding.

If you have feedback and want further clarification, or to challenge my thoughts, feel free to contact me.

My personal blog is available at *allanpresland.com*, and there is a raft of free resources available on the *Parenta* website, *Parenta.com/resources*. You can contact me directly via *Twitter* *@AlPres* or via email *allan@Parenta.com*.

Everyone in childcare is aware of the enormous contribution the *Early Years* sector makes to the children in our care, to hard-pressed working parents and to local communities, as well as to society as a whole. Imagine how much more it could contribute if every childcare business was successful?

Allan Presland
Winter 2016
PS: Follow me on Twitter *@AlPres*

Chapter 1: Focus

"Steve Jobs insisted that Apple focus on just two or three priorities at a time. "There is no one better at turning off the noise that is going on around him," Cook said. "That allows him to focus on a few things and say no to many things. Few people are really good at that." Walter Isaacson

The *Parenta National Childcare Survey (2015)* highlighted the fragile nature of the Childcare sector. Confirmed by the *National Day Nurseries Association (2016)* report, almost half of providers are *not* expected to make a profit this year. This is a staggering statistic and one that should alarm everyone involved in the sector.

However, if you spin that statistic around, that means *half* of settings in the country *are* forecast to make a profit, some of them very healthy ones.

This book details what the successful settings do that the less successful ones don't, by looking at each of the key areas within the business.

Key Finding

The most successful settings think about childcare differently than those who are less successful.

They completely understand that they are running a

business first, and as such, every decision they make reflects the need for that business to be successful.

They intrinsically understand that the more successful and profitable they are, the more they can invest in better education for children, better facilities, better staff and of critical importance, better-paid staff.

- Are you expecting to be profitable this year with your childcare setting?
- Are you gaining the returns from your business that you expect?
- Is every part of your business working as effectively as it possibly can?

YOUR RESPONSIBILITY TO YOU

A few months ago, a customer of mine, who is the owner of an incredibly successful setting, wrote an article that was entitled *Why profit and outstanding Childcare aren't mutually exclusive.* The opening paragraph read as follows:

"Dare I mention the 'p' word? Will this article be judged in the first sentence? Does the sector really shy away from being proud to make a profit?"

And therein lies the problem. Too often, profit and quality childcare are seen as being mutually exclusive.

But the problem goes further still. Who are owners of childcare business actually working for? Many see this as parents. Some as staff. Others as the community.

And yet all of these sentiments are wrong.

From a purely legal perspective, a company's number one responsibility is not to the customer, but to the shareholder. It doesn't mean customers aren't important, they are. But the people who invest and risk their money own it - not the employees, not the suppliers, not the customers, and not the community.

And whilst many reading this statement will disagree, there is a fundamental truth that must resonate with owners of childcare settings. For it is they who have taken the risk to set-up their Childcare centre or nursery, and they who pay the ultimate price if it fails.

It is critically important then, that owners aren't nervous or shy about making profits from childcare.

You are, first and foremost, running a business. You are one of Britain's celebrated entrepreneurs.

And in doing so, you put your personal and professional life on the line.

Too many people, particularly in this sector, see profit as greed. Look up greed in the dictionary. It's defined as an act of selfish desire. There is a huge difference between selfishness and self-interest, they are totally different. It is appropriate to maximise your reward given you have taken significant risk.

Those settings who are successful do everything in their power to maximise the profitability of their setting. They do this as they know they must continue to invest in their building and infrastructure as well as in staff development and staff pay, in systems and, critically in rewarding their shareholders, which so often is themselves.

This book explains how to make your setting more profitable.

FOCUS ON WHAT NEEDS TO CHANGE

So let me start by relaying the story of my very first experience of the sector. The first nursery I ever went to was in Bristol. The year was 1997 and the setting belonged to a friend of mine.

It was long before my wife and I had even thought of children, and so the whole concept was quite strange to me.

I was working at the time as a director of a large multi-national manufacturer running the service division and had been invited out to lunch by one of my colleagues. He asked to *pick my brains* due to the fact that I had just turned around our division from the worst performing of 20 across Europe to the best, within 18 months.

His wife, Sally, had a small nursery school which she loved. Apparently, it had always been a dream of hers to have her own nursery. She had worked in one since their children were small and a few years before, the opportunity had come up to purchase the business she currently worked in.

"How brilliant" they had thought; she knew the business well, she got on very well with all the 'girls' and the parents would know her too!

The reality had become very different. It wasn't going well, and it was now starting to affect their relationship on many levels. He asked me if I would look at their business and give them some ideas about how to make it better.

I made an appointment to go down to see them. I had spoken to Sally on the phone and I could tell she was uncomfortable talking to me. Who was I to help her?

I had the address and in 1997, before the wonders of *SatNav*, I set off with my trusty AA route planner along the M4 to Bristol to take a look.

Now, I'm from Bristol and although I have an understanding of the suburb where they were, when I arrived in what I thought was the right place I spent an hour trying to find the nursery, finally resorting to phoning and asking directions; turns out I was in the right place, just there was no signage to announce the nursery!

I was greeted by them both and went in and looked around.

At the time, I knew nothing about running a Childcare setting but I knew about running a business, and specifically about turning them around.

I have a vivid memory of how run-down the building looked from the outside though I recall the inside was clean and tidy, and so I asked her what she felt were the problems she faced.

Sally started saying repeatedly that it was all so hard. She was struggling to pay bills, 'the girls' didn't treat her the same, the rent was too high and she was behind paying her payroll taxes. She also said she'd never taken a salary from the business since she bought it. By this time she was sobbing!

My colleague raised his eyes at all of this. I could only imagine how it was affecting them both. They clearly had money worries and were investing a huge amount of time into the business.

"Right, I said, let's get down to basics".

I asked how full she was. (I didn't know the term *occupancy* at the time). She didn't really know though she thought about 60%.

I asked how many new children she had starting over the next quarter (I was still in the corporate mindset where everything was based on quarters of the year!) Not many she told me even, though she had a *'Good' Ofsted* rating of which she was really proud.

As I delved further, it looked like they were losing around £2,000 a month, though the accounts were all over the place, and it was difficult to get a real picture.

So I asked her, "What do you spend most of your time doing?"

She told me organising and motivating the staff though this was a problem as they still considered her their mate!

She also spent a huge amount of time preparing for the next *Ofsted* visit as she was determined to get an *Outstanding* grade.

She was working every day in the nursery. She spent time engaging with parents or *keeping them happy* as she put it, as that too was what she had been used to doing before.

I asked, "When do you focus on the business?"

"Every day," Sally replied. I'm here every day looking after the business"

"No, the actual business. When do you focus on improving the business, not on looking after *the girls* or parents or *Ofsted*? When do you look at the business?"

"What do you mean?"

"Well, marketing for a start. How do you promote your business? How do you find new parents? Why is there no signage to direct both me and parents so that they know you are here? How do you know all the parents are paying you? How do know you are charging the right amount?"

"I don't have time for all of that. I'm too busy running the nursery!"

I asked if I could recommend a few things to her, some tools to try. I suggested that she start with three things. Focusing on getting more children, getting someone to help her with the books so she knew what was happening, and concentrate on ensuring that she was getting paid. We then spent a few hours talking about how to solve these issues.

My friend and Sally seemed relieved. They had some direction, and I think just sharing the problem had helped. She obviously loved her work with the children; it was her vocation but she was clearly in over her head on the business.

We shook hands, and off I went. Driving back along the M4 I dwelt on the dilemma this couple found themselves in. Having no education or experience in running a business, verses running a nursery, they were focusing on what they understood, rather than what was needed.

Six months later, I was down that way visiting family so arranged to pop over and see them.

"Now that's easier to find," I thought as I pulled into the car park, referring to the three newly printed signs that shouted loudly at me as I arrived at the nursery.

"Thank you!" Sally said, "One of the parents is a printer, it was easy in the end!"

We went in, and she proudly showed me her accounts, happy in the knowledge that she now felt comfortable to answer my 'difficult' questions.

She went on to tell me that she now had more children attending and she was looking for more staff to cope with the increased workload.

She said the biggest problem was getting fees paid on time; a problem, which she hated dealing with, but she was trying. And whilst money was still incredibly tight, she did feel that things were moving forward and she knew what she had to do to keep improving.

I continued to meet up with this couple every few years. Three or four years after our first meet, they had moved from the old premises into a large Victorian building, increasing their capacity and a few years after that they had opened a second school. Clearly, business was beginning to thrive.

We caught up properly over dinner in 2005 by which time I had changed my career too. I was keen to find out what had been happening, and they were excited to tell me their news.

Their two settings had become the best in the area; they were full and had waiting lists for both. More importantly for them, they had an offer from a larger nursery chain to buy them which they were 'thinking' over.

I asked, "What changed it all, then?"

I remember she looked me in the eye and replied: "I started to focus on the business".

"Instead of just looking after the children, I looked after my business."

What happened to Sally is so often repeated with settings that I've visited. For those with a more vocational background, the focus is so often on the *care* and not the business. And it's not hard to see why, given care is often their area of expertise and people, naturally, gravitate to the areas they feel comfortable with. But it is the business that often needs attention, especially given that 49% of settings are forecast to be unprofitable this year.

FOCUS ON WEAKEST LINK

Oddly, 1997 was interesting for me for another reason also. My favourite business author, Eliyahu Goldratt, published his second book, *Critical Chain*. Goldratt is my favourite business author because his first book, *The Goal*, explains so much about making business a success.

Within *Critical Chain*, Goldratt drew the analogy of a chain to how a business works.

A chain, as we all know, has only one weakest link, and therefore strengthening any part of the chain, other than the weakest link, has no value whatsoever. A chain can only fail at its weakest link.

Goldratt highlighted that businesses are not dissimilar. Many business owners spend time, energy and effort making each part of their business better. They've seen this approach in great sporting events like the *Olympics* or *Formula 1*, as teams strive to shave weight from their bikes, boats, or cars to save time. This rarely works in business, however, particularly service businesses.

Back to the chain analogy, it's only through improving the weakest link that significant improvements can be made. The point here is the flow of products or services, or more appropriately, money, is constrained by that weakest link.

Therefore, investment in improvements anywhere other than the weakest link don't improve the overall performance of the business. The flow of money through the business is constrained by the weakest link and improvement must occur here if it's to have an impact on the whole business.

I see this issue re-enacted so often within the childcare sector. Much like Sally, many setting owners and managers continue to improve the care they provide, even though it's already good, yet neglect to focus on the actual business side of what they do.

More successful settings, however, have realised that *Good enough* is *Good enough*.

They have a *Good* regulatory body grading, and the care they provide is, actually, very good. They need then to now focus on making the business itself, very good too. Then they can go back and work on increasing the regulatory body grade.

And that means addressing the weakest link. The area where you can get the biggest bang for your buck; the area where you can have the greatest impact.

In the less successful settings, it's very often occupancy that's the biggest issue. With excess capacity being wasted, the easiest way to become more profitable is to increase occupancy, which in effect means working on your marketing and conversion processes.

FOCUS ON WHAT YOU CAN CONTROL

Of equal importance, though, is focusing only on those things which are within your control. Currently in England, we are about to move from 15 hours per week of State funding for childcare to 30 hours a week. Sounds great doesn't it, and it would be if the Government were buying services at what was perceived to be a fair rate, but the hourly rate paid by the State is seen to be below cost for the majority of providers, and understandably, most of the sector is in uproar.

At this point again there is a significant difference between how the most successful providers react to this change.

It is not within the scope of this book to debate the merits or the problems of this statutory change.

But there is a critically important point that separates the way highly successful settings are dealing with this issue against less successful settings.

Successful settings don't invest time and energy trying to fight against things that they can't control. Now that doesn't mean that I don't think the whole sector should be dealing with this issue, I do. But at a sector level.

But as an individual setting, focusing your attention on things that you can't control has no value. Better, follow the lead of the successful settings and find a way to either live with things you can't control or find a way to turn them to your advantage.

CONCLUSION

Successful settings often have a different mindset from other settings in the sector. They recognise that first and foremost, they are commercial businesses. As such, it is fundamental for them to maximise their profitability. In doing so, they know they are able to provide better care and provide better terms for staff.

Successful settings also always focus on the area of the business which will have the biggest leverage. They recognise that managing this weakest link, or bottleneck, will have the biggest impact on their business. Once addressed, they move on to the next area with the highest leverage.

Lastly, successful businesses in general, do not invest effort in worrying about things which are beyond the span of their control. Instead, they find ways to circumvent such issues.

KEY POINTS

1. **Successful settings focus sufficient time on the commercial side of their business.** They understand that doing anything less jeopardises the business as a whole, and therefore they must ensure that the business is working effectively to ensure it thrives.

2. **Successful settings recognise the need to work on the area of the business which is constraining it,** and that making areas which are not the constraint more effective does not improve profitability. The weakest link is the area which has the biggest impact on success.

3. **Successful settings do not worry about those things which are beyond their control.** They concentrate only on things they are able to control and learn to live with or navigate around such items.

Al's Rant

I subscribe to a publication that lists all the businesses in the UK that go into administration or liquidation, every day. I am truly shocked by the number of children's nurseries I see in the listing. There is at least one every few weeks. This is a tragedy for those whose lives are affected; not just the owners, but also the staff, children and families. But worse, it's a disaster for the sector. I do hope, with this book, we can, at least stem the flow of such occurrences.

This book highlights why it doesn't have to be this way. And if things really are that bad, please speak to me before you speak to an insolvency practitioner. We have solutions that can help and you have nothing to lose having a conversation!

CHAPTER 2: VISION AND VALUES

*"Company culture is present
whether you have planned for it or not." Unknown*

The *Parenta National Childcare Survey* showed that all profitable settings had one thing in common. They all had shared Vision and Values.

Key Finding

The most successful settings had taken the time to discuss and agree their vision and values. They lived and breathed them. The Values were written within staff handbooks, displayed on walls, explained in brochures and highlighted on websites. Every member of staff knew what was expected of them, where they were going and why.

The most profitable settings had not only set aside time to articulate their vision and values, but they had also integrated them into their business.

- Do you have a Vision for your business?
- Does every member of staff know the journey you are taking them on?
- Does everyone in your team know the values of the business and how to make decisions based on those values?

LEADING THE JOURNEY

Running a profitable business is about *selling;* even a childcare business.

Selling is so often seen as a negative, born of the days of double-glazing salesmen with their foot in the door. But that shouldn't be so today. Selling is about informing, influencing and reassuring.

Within your setting, you have to sell constantly. You have to sell your way of looking after children to parents and your way of doing things to staff.

But how do you do this if your own vision and your values are not clear to you, let alone to anyone else?

Our survey discovered that one of the biggest issues for owners was managing staff. We'll talk about how to recruit, engage, manage and motivate staff in later chapters, but this is where staff management starts; creating a vision that your staff can buy into, and values that they can respect and use as a framework for decision making. These issues also directly affect how you market your business and one of the key tenets of this book is to show you how to get your childcare setting full. Without the building blocks of *Vision and Values,* this objective will be difficult to achieve.

The reality for any business is that your staff define how successful you are. Many will say; "We're a childcare business. Our values are obvious, it's about the welfare and education of the children in our care" or some such words.

But this misses the point entirely. Indeed, staff engagement directly affects revenues and profitability and company culture is often cited as having a greater impact on success than company strategy.

However, it's only the owner who can create the correct environment and culture for staff to thrive and become engaged. If staff are engaged with your setting, motivated by what they want to do and passionate about their roles, your setting can only succeed.

To achieve this aim, though, you must have defined your *Vision and Values* first.

Your staff are the ambassadors for your business. And yet they can't be if they do not know the journey you are all on together or the framework for making decisions.

IT STARTS WITH WHY

Every childcare owner knows WHAT they do. Whilst there are lots of semantics, the basic premise is to educate early year's children.

Every childcare owner knows HOW they do it. You'll have a set of systems and processes that drive HOW you educate children. However, few childcare providers understand or are able to articulate WHY they do what they do.

This premise of WHY comes from the work of Simon Sinek from his book, *Start With Why: How Great Leaders Inspire Everyone To Take Action*. Why not, take the time to watch Sinek's *TED talk* where he explains his *Golden Circle* (WHAT, HOW, WHY) on *YouTube*, as he presents his concepts really well.

Sinek's book explains that WHY is about your purpose or belief. Once you understand this notion, it's easier for you to explain and communicate this to your market, your customers and your staff.

Sinek believes most organisations are not communicating their mission correctly. He argues that this happens because organisations communicate their mission *from the outside in* when they should be doing so *from the inside out*.

Sinek uses the example of *Apple* to illustrate his thinking. He states that if *Apple* was any other company, they would introduce themselves something like:

"We make great computers. They are beautiful designed, simple to use and user-friendly. Want to buy one?"

Sound familiar? Think *Dell, Sony, Lenovo, HP*. Instead, *Apple* actually say:

> *"We believe in challenging the status quo.*
> *We think differently. We put a lot of time into the products*
> *we create. Hi, we're Apple. We make computers".*

This approach is clearly different.

And as a result, they are able to charge premium prices for the products, and in some instances, they dominate market segments. Would you have bought an MP3 player from *Dell* or *HP*? No, you had an *iPod*.

The underlying message here is that Sinek explains that in their marketing most companies pitch their products (WHAT) and neglect to tell their prospects WHY they do what they do.

And so back to childcare.

WHY you do what you do is an important way of explaining how you differentiate yourself from your immediate competitors. Whether it's offering French lessons or sports lessons into your curriculum or having the highest number of graduates in your area, your WHY is an important building block to positioning your business to both your staff, prospects and existing parents.

Rather than:

- *What:* Educating Children.
- *How:* Using top quality staff and with passion.
- *Why:* To improve the lives of the youngest generation.

Childcare owners should communicate the other way around:

To improve the lives of the youngest generation (WHY) we employ top quality, passionate staff (HOW) to educate children (WHAT).

As an example, at *Parenta*, our WHY is to improve the business of childcare and upskill the childcare workforce.

We have many products and services which support nursery businesses and the childcare workforce, but underlying all of these products is our desire to help the *Early Years* sector. With 49% of settings not expecting to make a profit, we see it as critical that more support be provided to assist those who are struggling. That means more education to the workforce as a whole, as well as industry-leading products that enable settings to become more successful. As more settings become profitable, so they are able to invest in their staff, their infrastructure and ultimately the children, so that, in the end, we are all, working together for our children.

YOUR VISION

Once you fully understand your WHY, you need to be able to explain your vision.

Your vision is the end point of the journey you are taking with your staff and customers. Working without a vision is like getting into your car for your summer holidays and just driving having no idea where you're headed. The result is you end up driving around, wasting a lot of time and not actually getting to where you want to go.

You can't expect your staff to be pulling in the same direction as you if they don't know their destination!

So, it's down to you to define the vision of your business.

What's a vision?

It's not as mystical or *out there* as it sounds. A vision, quite simply, is a picture of what success will look like at a particular time in the future.

It encompasses answers to an array of questions such as:

- What does our organisation look like?
- How big is it?
- What are we famous for?
- Why does anyone care about what we do?
- How do people who work here feel about their jobs?
- How do you, as the founder, feel about the business?
- What's your role in it?

Complete the visioning process, and you'll have a clearly articulated end goal for your organisation - something that won't change every time the market or your mood shifts.

The vision though should be yours, the business owner. This is one of the few things that you should consider creating on your own. It's about what you want to say to the world.

It's about what you want to achieve.

Your *Vision Statement* should provide a sense of aspiration and stretch the imagination. A good vision statement will help inform direction and set priorities while challenging you and your staff to grow. It's also important that the vision statement is compelling to all of your staff.

As an example, *Parenta's* vision is:

> *"A world in which every child is loved
> and achieves their potential."*

We translate this idea to our customers by striving to provide leading products and services that can make a difference to how they run their childcare settings. We translate it to the sector by providing free information and resources.

For our staff, we have transformed our business into an *Limited Liability Partnership (LLP)*.

Within a LLP, staff are members or partners, rather than employees, and therefore share in the success of the business, much like in *John Lewis*. This means that they too, share in our combined success.

Lastly we translate it into a source for good via our charity, the *ParentaTrust*, which is committed to building ten nursery schools in post-conflict East Africa within ten years.

Now, clearly, our vision is, ultimately unobtainable. But that's not the point.

The point for a vision is simply to set direction. In our case, it set the direction that led to the free industry resources, our transformation to an LLP to benefit our staff and the setting up of our charity.

So in determining your vision, aim big and aim bold!

Here are five tips to keep in mind:

- When describing goals, project at least five to ten years in the future.
- Dream big and focus on success.
- Use the present tense.
- Infuse your vision statement with passion and emotion.
- Paint a graphic mental picture of the business you want.

After the vision statement is complete and finalised, your staff will have a clear idea of your vision for the company. You'll need to explain it to them, and ensure they understand the journey you'll be taking them on.

It's up to you to nurture and support that vision each day and to inspire your staff to do the same. With your support and dedication, you can empower your staff to fulfill the goals outlined in your vision statement.

To this end then, simply sticking your vision on the wall is not good enough. You need to live and breathe it every day so that staff understand it implicitly.

YOUR VALUES

The third and final component for setting the building blocks to increased profitability is to clearly define your values.

Your values are the framework which you and your staff should use to make all of your decisions.

Few smaller settings though have defined values, they tend to believe that this is the domain of large groups or chains. So whilst you as the business owner or manager may know what you expect of your staff, my experience suggests that few staff know the _values_ of the setting.

Many companies see no real value in having values (if you'll pardon the pun). My experience suggests the exact opposite. Each of us has a different personal value-set from our upbringing which have been honed to create the person we are today. If we all use these values for our decision-making and for our service delivery then we can only create an inconsistent level of service. What's needed is a common framework from which every member of staff can draw on.

As the setting owner, you need every member of staff to be acting in the same (pre-determined) way as decisions are made, to ensure you are delivering a superior level of service.

Again, the responsibility here lies with you. It's your responsibility to ensure that every member of staff understands the values that you have defined for your company, and can live by them.

If you have yet to define your values, you should consider how you want your staff to represent your company, and create between three and six values, which should describe how staff should operate.

PARENTA'S VALUES

For *Parenta*, this was a relatively easy exercise. Long before *Parenta*, I was the Service Director of a major manufacturer. I consider that Customer Service is in my blood, so for me, a key element of our values is customer delight. However, delighting customers can be difficult with a software product, as it has to be plural. For instance, it is not effective to create some functionality that one setting wants, as it might disrupt the needs of several settings.

Our second value is about people. I passionately believe that it's the people who determine each company's success.

Thirdly, it's about creating and consistently delivering quality. And lastly, it's about constantly adapting our portfolio of products and services to meet the needs and challenges of our marketplace.

This gave us the following set of core values: *Exceptional People, Customer Delight, Constant Innovation* and a *Commitment to Quality*.

We translated this into the following commitment:

Exceptional People
Providing
Customer Delight
Through
Constant Innovation
And
A Commitment to Quality.

Once defined, your values need to be constantly reinforced to your staff, and you'll need to ensure that you comply with them at every juncture. Your staff certainly won't do this if you don't.

In defining values, here are a few of the lessons I have learned:

- Just like any other group of people, a setting benefits from having clear values to define itself and guide behaviour.
- There comes a point in most organisations' growth where tacit assumptions are shared, and founding beliefs need to be made more formal and explicit. This particularly occurs when a childcare organisation becomes multi-sited.
- Writing values down as memorable phrases helps to make them more explicit, and using your own unique voice and phraseology helps to make them more real.
- Reinforcement is of huge value to the integration of your values – repeat, reward and, most importantly of all, recognise.
- Good, honed values can truly help make decisions. Especially the hardest decisions where numbers and analysis alone can't give you the answer and you have to think through more intangible factors.
- Modeling behaviour based on the values is crucial – especially for anyone in authority, starting with you and your management team. If you don't lead, the values will not stick.
- Be ready to be tested. On occasion employees should - and will - call you out based on your values. Whilst a bit painful, this is really positive because it means your values have really taken hold at a root level and are being used effectively.
- Values can often be a source of organisational pride.

Taking the time to define values, breathe life into them, personally exemplify them and keep them fresh and essential is one of the most important things you can do to make your setting thrive.

Once again, values have to be driven from the top-down. If you don't believe and act in the manner your values define, there is no likelihood that your staff will follow. You must constantly re-enforce them.

CONCLUSION

The most successful settings, those that perform better over time and are trading consistently profitably, have taken the time to articulate their vision and values and ensured that they are embedded within the culture of the business. In contrast, those without vision and values often fail to be profitable.

The most successful settings ensure that values are used to recruit staff, that values are used for decision-making and that values are used to determine marketing messages. Their values are integrated throughout the business.

Their marketing is based around the concept of WHY and highlights the hallmarks of what the business stands for.

Their vision gives clear direction and purpose to staff and provides clarity to customers.

KEY POINTS

1. **Your staff control how successful you are.**
   If they are engaged with your setting, motivated by what they want to do and passionate about their roles, your setting can only succeed. To do so, staff must have direction (Vision) and a framework for operating (Values).

2. **Clearly define your vision**, so that you and your staff clearly understand where you are headed and WHY.

3. **Articulate a vision which is audacious and bold.** Setting direction is key for everyone to know where they are going.

4. **Define your setting's values.** Embrace them. Live by them. Reference them at every opportunity.

5. **Ensure your values are displayed** throughout, in staff rooms, within internal newsletters, within customer newsletters, and on your website. They need to become an integral part of your culture.

Al's Rant

Too many settings are not focusing on the need to set direction and values. They consider setting visions and values as just for the big boys. It isn't and nothing could be further from the truth. Don't miss this fundamental step, you have nothing to lose.

Chapter 3: Marketing Your Setting

"Marketing is what gets you noticed." Rowan Atkinson

The second largest issue raised in the *Parenta National Childcare Survey* boiled down to *marketing*. It's interesting, though, that this it was often hidden in a variety of other comments such as, "How do I compete with the newer/bigger/posher/smarter nursery which has just opened up the road?"

Key Finding

The most successful settings have clearly defined customer acquisition strategies that ensure they are constantly full. They do this to maximise profitability at all times.

- Is your setting consistently full?
- Do you have marketing systems that ensure your setting is full throughout the year?
- Are you just relying on word of mouth to keep new customers coming to your door?

Unless your setting is running consistently full with no free spaces, these questions are fundamental to increasing your profitability.

MAXIMISING RESOURCES

My wife is a huge fan of the rock band *Queen*. A couple of years ago I took her to see *We Will Rock You* at a theatre in London. I'd seen the show many years ago and was impressed by the incredible vibrancy and the enthusiastic audience participation.

But this time it was different. There were loads of empty seats; I'd say the theatre was about half full. And this was on a Saturday evening at their peak time. With empty seats in every row, the atmosphere was different, the audience participation had changed. To be honest, compared to the previous showing, it was embarrassing!

Inevitably, the show closed shortly afterwards. It was no longer economically viable to run performances in a half empty theatre, as costs remain the same whether the theatre is full or empty.

And so it is for *Early Years* settings. The costs of running a setting at close to 100% capacity are not dissimilar to running it at 75% or 60%. Yes, you may need some extra staff, but the overall overhead remains, irrespective of how full you are.

The key point is this: Running your setting at anything less than close to 100% occupancy is simply costing you money.

Now, many owners will say, "That's obvious, I already know that". And yet, I constantly attend settings where I hear sentences like, "I'm full, my occupancy is 75%". And when challenged, they answer that surveys say the average occupancy is about 75%, and they are about the same level.

These are not the same sentences.

One is talking about *average occupancy*, the other it about *occupancy maximisation*.

CUSTOMER ACQUISITION PROGRAMME

This means that you must have a clearly defined method of attracting new prospects to your setting so that you are always full and ideally have a waiting list.

Why do I use the term *Customer Acquisition Programme?* Because successful businesses think of bringing in new customers as a process. If your occupancy is less than 90% you are not focusing enough attention on how you acquire new customers.

Successful settings recognise that an effective customer acquisition programme is *the most* important aspect of running their business as this has the biggest impact firstly on sustainability and then profitability.

These programmes are switched on at certain predetermined times of the year, or when occupancy is forecast to fall to ensure that a steady stream of prospects are always attracted to their door.

For instance, a client of mine regularly starts their advertising campaign for their July intake in January to ensure that those thinking of childcare are aware of their offering way in advance.

But the key month in the above sentence is not January, it's July.

Most settings tend to consider their new intake as being for September. Not this setting, they work hard to ensure that new children start in July to ensure that occupancy, and, therefore, revenue does not take a dip in August.

And to further highlight the point, to start their advertising campaigns in January, the planning starts at the end of November. Nothing is left to chance for this setting to ensure they are always full.

And *full* means greater than 98%.

WHY IS MARKETING SO IMPORTANT?

So many nurseries believe advertising is all the marketing they need. Marketing and advertising are not the same. Marketing is an ongoing process to engage customers so they are aware of your setting and believe it's a suitable place to investigate for their child.

You can then connect with parents via a phone call and arrange to show them around.

Advertising is just about raising awareness. It is not the process by which you *create* new customers, though it is the process where you *interest* new customers.

So, the first part of the marketing journey is to create a steady stream of high-value prospects to your door, so you can convert them into customers.

If you do not have effective marketing systems in place the following will occur:

- You will lose revenues and your profit margins will decrease. If your nursery is below the average occupancy rate your marketing systems are simply not working.
- Your competitors will end up *catching* the most lucrative parents, especially that bright shiny nursery just around the corner. If you enjoy watching them thrive whilst you work so hard, then don't implement a marketing system!
- You will always be reactive to the occupancy needs of your setting.

By contrast, a marketing system will ensure that you have a constant and continual flow of new parents to your door.

Quite simply, not having a well-oiled marketing machine that constantly brings you new customers means your business cannot thrive.

CAPACITY WASTED

Often when you go to a doctor's surgery there is a sign saying how many wasted appointments there were at the doctors in the previous month. Doctors want to highlight the amount of capacity that is wasted by patients who fail to attend booked appointments. In this instance, it is clear that those appointments are lost forever. They are simply wasted.

Do you measure the wasted capacity in your setting?

I am always surprised about how few childcare providers measure their wasted capacity.

As with the doctor's story, once you have allowed a session to be wasted, *it is wasted forever*. If your margins are poor and you're not making the amount of money you would like to, almost certainly, you are wasting your capacity.

Having an effective marketing strategy is, therefore, essential to fill those wasted sessions and improve financial results, and measuring your wasted capacity in revenue terms will provide you with a startling reminder of how much additional revenue you could be generating.

The items within this chapter will explain how to ensure that your setting is full and how to ensure you have a waiting list.

WHAT IS MARKETING?

Marketing is one of those subjects everyone has a view on and yet no one really seems to know! I've been in marketing for over 25 years and it was only recently I found a definition that actually made sense. And now this new understanding has transformed how I want to run my businesses.

This definition comes from the author and speaker, Barnaby Wynter:

"Marketing is every interaction that affects the customer".

If that's the case, then marketing descends right through your organisation and touches every part of your customer experience. Marketing only ends at the point your customers leave you.

Before we go on to talk about customer experience in *Chapter 10*, let's focus on the value of enquiries.

WHAT'S THE VALUE OF A LEAD?

When I visit a setting, one of the first questions I ask is, "What's the value of a lead to you?"

The most successful settings always know the answer to this question, though the majority do not. And yet, it's one of the most important questions for any business to answer.

To work this out, you need to start with *Lifetime Customer Value (LCV)*.

LCV is the revenue received from a client for the duration of their time spending money with you. Don't forget, if the parents have more than one child, this figure would include the revenue for both (or more) children.

Let's go through an example.

For the sake of simplicity, let's make the numbers easy and assume that a full-time place at your setting is £1,000 per month. And then let's assume that you are open for 52 weeks per year, and there are no discounts for holidays.

This means that a full-time place has a revenue value to you of £1,000 x 12 months = £12,000 per year.

Now let's assume that, for your setting, your average placement is for four years. This means that the revenue from a typical full-time place is worth 4 x £12,000 = £48,000.

And that's before you have added any extras! Or any siblings!

According to the *Office for National Statistics (ONS)*, the average number of children per family in the UK is 1.7.

Now, if you multiply £48,000 x 1.7, the revenue value of a lead to you would be £81,700.

So, a lead for a full-time place, and assuming the child stays with you for four years and has the average number of younger siblings is worth over £80,000 to you!

Calculate your own LCV

Your average monthly revenue per child is £	A	
You are open for how many months per year	B	
The average duration for child at your setting	C	
Your LCV is A x B x C =	£	

The value of a lead is the total gross revenue spend over the lifetime of the customer.

The problem with this metric by itself is it can be misleading when looking at the revenue in a given period.

Personally, I prefer to look at the value of a lead over a given time period (say a year). That way, by looking at the revenue generated by new starts in a year, and dividing it by the number of leads in the year, you come to a more realistic number you can use to measure your costs of acquiring new business.

We do exactly this at *Parenta* as all of our products have recurring revenue (customers pay a small fee to use them each month).

When we consider the value of a lead, we look at the gross revenue in the period (one year) and not the revenue generated for the future. (We are privileged in that we lose very few customers, and as such many have been with us for more than 12 years. In which case, it's difficult to assume a customer lifetime duration).

So, in this case, you'll need to take the total revenue generated by new starts in the period and divide it by the number of enquiries you have received. You are then able to determine the cost of a lead.

The 2016 *NDNA* report tells us that average occupancy for a nursery was running at 72%. It's, therefore, easy to see how much extra revenue you could generate if you could fill those remaining 28% of places.

This means you should be devoting a huge proportion of your efforts to constantly marketing your nursery to increase occupancy.

COST PER ENQUIRY

Now let me ask you how much you actually pay for a lead? In most instances, it's very little.

The cost of an enquiry is hard to measure. Worse, having asked many marketers this question I was surprised that there is little agreement.

The *Department for Education's (2015) Review of Childcare Costs: The Analytical Report,* suggests that word of mouth (provider's reputation) is the main reason for choosing a provider for 65% of parents.

Many see these leads as free and yet in a real sense they are not. These leads are generated from how your existing customers perceive your delivery.

We'll talk about the need to ensure your customer experience is exceptional in *Chapter 5*, but this is one of the key places where investment in customer experience has an indirect impact. For those leads you do have to pay for, you need to know the cost per lead.

So take the total number of leads you have generated in a period and divide by the costs associated with generating these leads, for each marketing channel.

This is your cost per enquiry. Don't forget to monitor and trend these metrics.

As long as the cost per lead is less than the revenue per lead, you're onto a winner.

COST PER SALE (COST PER NEW CUSTOMER)

The last key metric you need for leads is the cost per sale. Again this is a simple metric to calculate. It's simply the cost of your advertising and marketing in a given period divided by the number of customers that register at your setting.

MEASURING YOUR ENQUIRIES

One of the most surprising statistics from the *Parenta National Childcare Survey* was how few settings accurately measure their enquiries or leads.

A lead is an enquiry from anyone about your business. You should have sufficient systems in place to ensure that *every* lead is captured – you'd be surprised how many nurseries don't do this.

Measuring where your leads come from and which ones convert is fundamental to ensuring you are effectively optimising your marketing investment.

It is a prerequisite to improving your profitability, as it enables you to know where to continue investing to get the best return. For instance, without this data, you wouldn't know if, say, your leaflet drops were more effective than your *Google AdWords*. With the information, you might decide to stop leaflet drops and increase your spending with *Google*.

YOUR ENQUIRY FUNNEL

I was recently in a meeting with the MD and marketing manager of a Top 20 chain of nurseries. During the meeting, the marketing manager produced a list of the leads generated by her team as we were discussing the occupancy of each setting. There was much concern as the occupancy rates were not where they should be.

What became interesting was how the marketing manager kept insisting that she was doing her job well, as she had generated lots of leads, but she felt the setting managers had not followed them up properly.

We started to dig into the data, and a pattern emerged that was not to her liking as many of the leads were not *suitable* for the individual settings. For instance, some were completely out of area, some for services not offered (such as after-hours or weekend care), others for mums who were newly pregnant and were enquiring about the future.

The point here is that all leads do not have the same value. The ones quoted above are all valuable in either telling you what additional services are required and where, or for keeping in touch until the time is right. But they are not what we refer to as *Marketing Qualified Leads (MQLs)*.

MQLs are those leads that are 100% relevant to your business because they fit your criteria for turning them into customers.

In the story above, we had to stop and define what constituted an *MQL* before we re-ran the data.

In doing so, about 25% of the leads were removed and suddenly the story being presented by the marketing manager changed and she realised that she had more work to do in producing quality leads.

To make sense of this, marketers use an enquiry funnel which demonstrates how leads move through a marketing and sales system. This also identifies where efforts should be focused to ensure you have the right number of new customers, at the right time.

You should be checking your enquiry funnel each week, and adapting your marketing process to address any weaknesses.

An enquiry funnel for childcare should look something like this.

To clarify this funnel, a lead is an enquiry from anyone about your business. You should ensure that you have systems in place to ensure that *every* lead is captured, something that many settings do not do!

As explained a *Marketing Qualified Lead* is a term used by larger companies to identify a lead as appropriate to pass to their sales team.

It is still completely relevant though, even to owner-managed childcare settings, as it allows you to differentiate relevant leads from those for services you don't offer.

Leads that don't make the *MQL* pot identify a market need that you are not currently offering.

The remaining four items are self-explanatory.

UNDERSTANDING YOUR COMPETITION

Having an idea of what other local childcare providers are doing is the key to helping you win the business of parents needing childcare.

In much the same way the supermarkets keep tabs on their competitors' pricing– knowing your rivals' strengths and weaknesses will make a big difference when a parent asks why they should choose your setting.

Step 1 – Do some recon

There will be a few key performance points you will want to measure to see how your competitors stack up against what you offer, namely

- The price they charge per child.
- What's included in their service.
- Do they offer any extras (like snacks).
- What their facilities are like.

Now, try to think like a parent looking for a childcare provider. What do you think would be most important to them? Is there anything that would really sway their decision if two settings offered exactly the same thing and were similarly priced? If you aren't sure what factors would play a part in their decision, ask some of your existing parents why they chose your setting in the first place.

Step 2 – Arm yourself with the facts

Gathering information about other local childcare providers is an easy process. Start with two or three nurseries and track their activities in detail.

This can be done by:

- Typing their name into a search engine and seeing what comes up.
- Visiting their website.
- Subscribing to their newsletter so you get updates on their activities.
- Joining their page on *Facebook*.
- Following them on *Twitter*.
- Browsing through the photos on their website.
- Stopping by their setting and asking for a brochure.

Once you become familiar with the nurseries you choose to research, write a list of strengths and weaknesses you think they have.

Step 3 – Be the best in battle

When parents are looking around your setting for the first time don't be afraid to ask them what other childcare providers they have visited locally to build up a picture of whom you're up against. If you know that a certain competitor is open for fewer hours, then you could highlight the additional flexibility you offer, should the parents need more sessions in the future. This may prompt the parents to notice the weakness at the other setting, without you having to openly criticise.

Whatever happens, though, never criticise a competitor.

UNIQUE SELLING POINTS

Unique Selling Points (USPs) are those features that set you apart from the competition. Consider what you offer against what your competition offers and focus on these points as your *USPs*.

This could be that you are the only *Outstanding* setting in your local area, or you have the highest number of graduates or anything else that explains how you are different.

DRIVING NEW ENQUIRIES

There are two prime ways successful settings drive new enquiries and three or four secondary ways. The two primary ways are from referrals and websites, and the secondary are via *Google Adwords/Facebook* ads, leaflets drops, and radio adverts.

No surprises there you may say? But few settings use any of these options effectively. The ones that do though are very successful.

Before we talk about the lead generation systems, though, let's start with the basics; your setting needs to look smart, as, like it or not, first impressions matter!

The number of settings I visit where there's a shabby sign on the outside of the building is worrying. I'm sure the signage looked great ten years ago, but now it looks drab and unkempt: not good enough if you want to appeal to new customers. Likewise the front of the building, the garden and the car park. You need to consider the appeal of the whole setting; how does it look, how does it sound, how does it smell?

Overall, how does it feel?

As an example, I was stuck in traffic the other day somewhere on the South-coast and drove past a nursery with a very simple sign, elegant in design, modestly proclaiming the name. The signage instantly caught my eye. It was clear and professional, modern and clean. Without even seeing the building (it was hidden by hedges), meeting the owner and staff, or reading anything about them, I instantly had the impression that this was a quality establishment - just from the signage!

Compare this to a nursery I drive past regularly. The sign looks at least 20 years old. The name is hand drawn (not by a professional sign-writer) and is decorated with faded flowers and faded teddy bears on it.

It looks dated. If I'm really honest, it looks quite sad!

Would I be interested in sending my three-year-old to this setting? No, I wouldn't even consider it. It might have the best staff, the best facilities, the best building and internals, and maybe even the best *Ofsted* report; and yet, the signage gives me no confidence that this is a quality establishment.

The worse part is the cost of a new sign is inexpensive. With websites like *VistaPrint*, you can have new, modern, engaging signage from about £50.

Step back and approach your setting tomorrow with a new pair of eyes. Does it look fresh, smart, bright and professional? If not then why would potential customers be interested in even talking to you?

YOUR WEBSITE

If 65% of all new enquiries come from word of mouth, what's the next most important aspect of marketing for parents to find your setting? Well, it will come as no surprise to learn that the next strategy on the list, by a significant margin, is the internet.

Everyone nowadays has access, often via mobile, and most people use internet search as a key part of their day.

It's therefore, essential that you have a website and an effective one at that. A few pages that a parent created for you years ago that you haven't updated is again, simply not good enough.

You need a modern website that must work on a *smartphone* and is clearly current and shows that you care about your online presence. If it says, *"Welcome to our new website, June 2009"* you have a problem. You'd be surprised how many childcare websites do say something like this!

Many question the need for mobile compatibility however with over 50% of all searches now undertaken on a mobile device this is no longer an option. Your website must be fully mobile compatible.

Your website needs to contain vital, up-to-date information and bright and engaging pictures of children and staff.

Remember, your website must appeal to web-savvy customers who search other websites. In this online space, you are competing with all other dazzling, impressive websites out there, not just other child carers. People are used to accessing key information quickly and succinctly when they want it.

Pretty flying butterflies, and the font *Comic Sans* should be consigned to history. Bright, articulate, engaging are the style of websites today.

Your website needs to be optimised for Search Engines. Detailing *search engine optimisation (SEO)* is beyond the scope of this book, and to be honest, beyond the scope of most small business owners.

Your website company will be able to assist you with this.

You also need testimonials from your customers on your website. Nothing proves quality better than feedback from other customers. If you want proof, just think how the hospitality industry relies on the feedback from sites like *Trip Advisor.*

Once you have the basics correct, your website should have clear *calls to action (CTAs)*. A *call to action* is a request for the user to do something.

A critical mistake is to have a website that provides all of your unique selling points and then hides a telephone number in the *Contact Us* page. A *CTA* is essential to entice your customer to do *something*.

The best *CTAs* entice the customer to book an appointment immediately. But this is notoriously difficult to get right. It's like asking someone to get married having just met them in a bar; that's a lot of commitment early in your relationship!

It might be better, and slightly more successful when in a bar to just ask for the phone number of your potential partner.

And so it's similar for websites. Don't ask for prospects to commit to providing you with all their information up front. You simply need to ask them for their mailing information so that you have permission to keep sending relevant information into their inboxes.

In the same way, don't ask for all the information about your prospect on *Day One*. It's likely to lead to a rejection; at this stage; name and email address is sufficient.

As you gather this information, you'll start to build one of the most important assets for the future of your business. You'll gain a list of potential clients who you can engage with (via email) on a regular basis.

Before we move off the subject of websites, a word of caution. There are a lot of companies who claim they will build you a *beautiful website*. If you want a beautiful website, for the sake of having a beautiful website, then buy from them.

If you want a website that will drive leads, find a website provider who understands how important this is, and will show you how they drive leads for their other customers.

As an example, one of our nursery customer's website regularly generates over 65 leads per month. Every month.

Now these are leads, not *MQLs*. But even so, if you have a 60-place nursery with average occupancy, that gets you full pretty quickly!

Another customer's website generates more traffic to the *Gov.uk* website children's section than the *NHS* or *Boots* or any other well-known brand. The administrators of *Gov.uk* were so impressed they emailed the nursery owner to congratulate her – she then forwarded the email to us as we built and manage the website.

It's a chain of three settings, but just think how many leads they must be getting if they are generating that much traffic.

You need the *right* website, not just *a* website.

LIST BUILDING

So before we talk about how to build a list let's discuss why we need to build a list. First the bad news.

No matter how good your website is, the vast majority of people will visit it once, and never return.

On average it takes between seven and 13 *touches* to drive a quality sales lead.

In this context, a touch is each time a prospect comes into contact with your brand. So, for example, this could be contact with your brand via:

- Website
- Video
- Emails
- Books
- Brochures or prospectuses
- Email ads
- *Google Ads* or *Facebook Ads*
- Signage
- Referrals
- Show rounds
- Etc.

So, you need to create a list of the email addresses of all those who come to your website and those who ring in, so that you can keep engaging with them or increasing your *touch* rate.

The good news is, when people do decide to buy, they buy from whomever they have some form of relationship with, and the reality is, you'll make far more money by using a list, than just having a website.

If you email your *list* every week with some valuable, interesting information (i.e., you have a relationship with them), *at the time they are ready to buy,* they are more likely to consider your services.

So, a list is the mechanism you use to ensure that your services are front of mind for all those who are considering childcare in your local area.

It is also a great mechanism to keep in touch with your existing customers, preventing the apathy that so often can occur with existing customers.

The other piece of good news here is, other than the time it takes you to create content each week, sending out relevant information to prospects is practically free.

Compare this to the cost of other media!

Traditional advertising, such as print and radio is expensive.

Your need to capture as many names and addresses of prospective clients as you possibility can and create and publish interesting and relevant content.

Once you have the system to stay in contact with prospects, you'll see a change in the way your enquiries engage with you.

The key here is to keep your offering at the front of mind and to show prospects why your setting is ideal for their child. More information about list building and systems for distributing your emails are available within the free resources section of the *Parenta* website.

If you are sending a large volume of emails though, don't use your normal email address and email system. You can easily be *blacklisted* by internet providers if they think you are sending *spam* emails. You may know that they're not *spam* but your email provider might not.

There are many commercial email providers available (*Google* email systems) at low costs. Use one of these!

Better still, these email systems have auto-responders, which send prescheduled emails to parents and prospects at predetermined times.

The big value here is that once it's set up, an auto-responder simply works. You don't have to do anything at all. Now whilst this may sound like a good thing, you need to be very careful.

Once you've set-up your auto-responder, it's tempting to just leave it. However, what if the message you're sending does not convert or drive more enquiries? The answer is you need to test all of your marketing messages, all of the time.

If you use the dashboard I propose in *Chapter 11*, you will have a clear track of all of your funnel metrics. Vary one item at a time within your funnel and see how enquiries respond. If it increases enquiries, brilliant, if it decreases them, then you'll need to revert back. The key point is you need to keep testing everything.

A list, however, as a mechanism to engage with prospects is not the objective. It is simply the means; a cog in the lead generation machine that you are creating. The end-point of this machine is to convert your list into paying customers.

BUILD THE RELATIONSHIP WITH PROSPECTS

We have already discussed the fact that people buy when they are ready to buy. And beyond that, people buy from people they know, like and trust.

So, within our emailing process, we are trying to build rapport with prospects which demonstrate your *USP* and your WHY so that you can demonstrate the uniqueness and quality of your setting. You might want to do this by telling the story about your business and why you do what you do.

Don't forget, people love stories and this adds a certain uniqueness and character to your email structure. Stories are also entertaining.

However, remember that quality beats quantity. You'll need to mix your marketing messages to ensure that you achieve the end–result of converting prospects to paying customers.

Sending out emails though is futile if they're not opened!

Just think of the hundreds of emails that you receive every day. Your emails are competing against every one of those emails for attention and so it has to stand out to ensure your message gets through.

So you need to ensure that the subject line grabs people's attention, and gives them an incentive to actually open the mail. Don't forget, people's time is valuable and you need to ensure you are providing something of value.

Finally, it's important to remember that building a list and building a relationship with prospects is the long game.

As mentioned, it's about keeping in constant touch with prospects so that when they are ready to buy, you are at the front of mind.

It's also about constantly reminding parents who have chosen another setting over yours, that you still exist, you still provide quality childcare, and most importantly of all, that you still care about them. It makes a difference.

HOOK, WHERE'S THE HOOK!

You need a hook. Not the type from Peter Pan, but a hook to entice people to give you their information. This hook can have many other names, dependent on which author you read. It may also be called an *Irresistible Free Offer (IFO)*, a *Lead Magnet* and sometimes even a *Gift*. They're all the same thing.

A hook, IFO or *Lead Magnet* is a gift for your prospects. It should be something of high-perceived value, but something that doesn't cost you much. A *guide* of some sort, provided it's well produced, is often used as a hook. Examples of guides could be:

- "A guide to choosing the right child care for you."
- "A parent's guide to settling in your child at nursery."
- "The parent's guide to the top attractions for under 4's in (local area)."
- "Why learning to speak French at pre-school will help your child's linguistic development."
- "The ten-step list to preparing for going back to work."

Create something unique to your nursery that has sufficient value to prospective parents to entice them to share their contact information.

The more content you produce the more you remain at the parent's front of mind, and provided you publish it on your website, the higher your *Google* ranking will rise.

Don't assume that all parents will be attracted by the same offer. They won't, but you know the main draw of your setting so write about this and ensure its value is laid out for parents to consider.

A stand alone website is insufficient these days. No longer just an online brochure, *a website is a mechanism for gaining permission to establish an online relationship with your prospects* so that you can continue to engage with them and they eventually come for a *show round* and become clients.

Don't forget, though, that your existing customers are still your largest marketing asset. So use the two concepts to further enhance your relationship with your existing parents. Interactive systems for parents to log onto your data system are important, as are systems that provide updates on how each child is progressing. (We'll talk about these systems later).

Equally, use the mailing mechanism to provide interesting and relevant information to all parents.

TESTIMONIALS

As discussed the most important aspect of marketing your business is the referrals from your existing customers.

If your customers love your service, then they're going to talk about it with their friends and colleagues and this will lead to the start of your enquiry process. If you are not getting regular referrals, then something is very wrong with the way people perceive your service. Referrals lead to increased revenues and increased profits. Make sure you have systems to record enquiries that come from referrals.

Within your marketing get as many testimonials from happy and supportive parents as possible; indeed in this context there really cannot be too many.

In a more traditional business, sometimes testimonials lack credibility and do more damage than good.

Not so for Childcare. The testimonial that mentions specific members of staff or specific aspects of your delivery has a huge impact on the perceived quality of your business. Indeed, studies have shown that a testimonial is over 20 times more credible than anything you say yourself.

Now, many settings I visit have testimonials available, sometimes on the wall or in books, but few have a large number, and often they are quite old. To busy staff, posting fresh testimonials seems to be a low priority.

So there are two things you need to do.

Firstly, you need to have a mechanism to collect testimonials, and secondly, you need to share them with prospective customers.

Let's focus on collecting testimonials first.

Now, I know it sounds obvious, but the best way to collect testimonials is to *ask for them*. Of course, you could ask for them directly, but this may be a little uncomfortable. An easier and far more effective solution is to build appropriate questions into your enrolment, leaving and on-going feedback systems.

If the care you provide is good you're going to start getting testimonials pretty quickly. However, if you move into the *WOW!* zone that we will discuss in *Chapter 5: Customer Engagement*, the testimonials will flow faster, and will be even more gushing.

Generating testimonials needs to be systematised, like so many other parts of your business.

Once a new child has started at your setting, after about two weeks, you need to ask the parents to complete a survey about how they have found the service so far, what went well (and what didn't) when they were inducted, how they felt about the initial show round, and most importantly, why they chose your setting.

Online survey systems are cheap to access, incredibly easy to set-up and a breeze for parents to use, so you should start here. Create your survey, have a number of quantifiable questions and allow for open-ended questions. This is where the most authentic testimonials will come from.

And send a similar survey (not the bit about how well you're doing) to those parents who didn't choose your setting. You'll need to add a friendly note asking for their time, and accept that you probably won't get too many back, but those you do get back should be treated like gold dust. And don't forget, if you followed the systems explained earlier you'll have their mailing information, so sending the questionnaire is easy.

Sending the questionnaire to parents who have not chosen your setting has massive benefits.

Firstly, it tells you why the competition is better/different from you and where parents are going.

Secondly, it shows the parents that you really care what they think. If you continue to mail them even though their children aren't within your enrolment, who do you think they'll think of if/when they're unhappy with the current setting? It's back to the engagement strategy we talked about earlier.

Make sure, when you write your surveys, that you guide your parents to give you valuable feedback. Do this by asking specific questions about some of the elements of your provision, especially your *Unique Selling Points*. It is this specificity that will give you the strongest and most valuable testimonials.

When displaying testimonials, on your website or in your setting ensure that you choose diverse aspects. A significant volume of testimonials reassures parents that your provision is well-liked by other parents, however, usually only the top few will be read.

So ensure that the top few cover several different aspects of what you do and mention several different members of staff.

Lastly, *always* seek permission from parents to use their testimonials. On surveys include a tick box to confirm you can use their comments and feedback. For letters and emails, always write and ask. This enables you to use real names. Make it better still by using photos of those parents. This provides even more credibility.

In conclusion, I strongly recommend that you leverage the role of your most loyal customer by asking them to provide lots of testimonials. If they are verifiable, and specifically endorse key aspects of your business in an honest and trustworthy way, people will respond to them.

Be aware that too few childcare owners provide multiple testimonials on their website. This is a huge mistake. Add all testimonials to your website. Every single one. And keep adding them. Weekly. Again, they won't all get read, but the power of this tactic on potential parents is immense.

And finally, ensure your customers are also adding testimonials to *Google Business*. This is really important and something most childcare businesses are missing. More about *Google Business* later in the chapter.

VIDEO TESTIMONIALS

In the technology age, digital testimonials really are the way to impress!

They move the testimonial up the ladder of authenticity to the top rung and have an amazing effect on your website's search engine rankings.

And they are so easy to do.

No-one expects super quality here; indeed, if the testimonial does look crafted it loses authenticity. Rather, just use the video function on your *smartphone* to capture what parents are saying (with their permission of course) and add it immediately to your website.

Better still, if you an abundance, create your own *YouTube* channel to share the glowing views your parents have about your service.

This works amazingly well. If you have loads of video testimonials, it's highly likely that prospective parents in your community will know one of those people talking about your service. As testimonials go, it doesn't get any better than that!

REFERRALS

A referred customer is far superior to the one brought in from *cold* advertising.

In fact, referrals from existing customer are the most valuable form of lead. Why? Because when someone else sells your services, they are always completely and totally believed.

People who refer are your secret sales force.

The problem is most customers don't know that you want referrals (why would they), and they don't know how to refer someone because most nurseries haven't implemented any systems to deal with referrals.

How many of your current customers came from referrals from other customers?

And that's the point, most settings don't know because they haven't measured. The referral strategy of most businesses looks something like this:

1. Hope.
2. Pray.
3. Do nothing about it.
4. Hope some more.
5. Complain that they never get referrals.

Like everything else, if you want referrals, you need to build a system to gain them.

The thing to note here is most of your parents have a huge capacity to refer. They often have dozens of friends with similar aged children. And what if every single one of your customers recommended one additional family? Just stop and think what your setting would look like and how long your waiting list would be if every family recommended just one other?

Equally, giving referrals deepens the commitment of the customer, which increases their propensity to spend with you.

There are two key systems for gaining referrals, those done on an ad-hoc, random basis and those created through a group event. Irrespective, both need to be systematised.

SINGLE REFERRALS

Single referrals are where a parent referrers other families, one at a time.

The obstacle with most customers in general, not just childcare, is they don't know the service provider wants referrals and they don't know how to make a referral.

Once these two points are understood, it's easy to adapt processes and systems to address these points.

Firstly, if you have vacancies, make it known in all your communication systems with families that you have space and are actively looking for new children to fill it. Better still, offer some form of referral incentive to parents as a thank you.

Secondly, have a system for parents to tell you they have referred someone. Add it as a page to your website, or devise a system for parents to drop you a note via your software's parent portal. Irrespective, it has to be incredibly easy to pass this information on.

Next, write to the prospective family, inviting them to tour your facilities, ensuring that you mention who they were referred by. If you have a group referral event coming up in the near future (see below) then giving them an exclusive invitation to that event works even better!

Assuming that you conduct the tour, and the parents do sign-up with you, make sure you send the original referrer *something* to acknowledge them giving you the lead, and, importantly, acknowledge them in your next newsletter. This is massively important, as it implicitly signals to your other customers that referrals are expected and welcomed.

The value of this approach to referrals is they become self-fulfilling. As a parent gets acknowledged, so another parent thinks they can do the same too.

Now, you will still need a quality website, so that the referred parent can do their own research, but successful settings find that referrals are usually both the cheapest and highest converting of all their leads.

GROUP REFERRAL EVENTS

The alternative to single referrals is to create group referral events. I've seen a number of settings use these very effectively. They do so by creating an air of exclusivity for the event by making it *invitation only* and holding an evening occasion, where they highlight the benefits of their setting to prospective parents.

The secret to these events is to use your existing customers as your secret weapon to attract their friends to showcase how good you are.

Start by promoting in your newsletter the *invitation-only* evening for new, or expecting parents, and asking your current parents if they know people they'd like to recommend.

It's important to imply exclusivity here, so you need to infer that there are a limited number of tickets.

Keep reminding existing parents of the event until you have enough prospective families committed. If necessary, you can provide a special offer incentive as part of the invitation to prospects and make it even more appealing by saying the offer only applies to the first five or so people to sign-up.

Make the event interesting and exciting, have super-smart staff on hand to answer questions, and give a quick intro speech explaining your values and vision and how these affect your method of delivering *Early Years*. Offer wine and soft drinks for guests on arrival, and serve an array of tasty nibbles.

In a large building have staff conduct tours on a one-family basis and ensure they have a script for describing your facilities.

Finally, make sure you are on-hand to speak to each family individually and that you have the tools and paperwork to sign-up parents on the spot. If it's a large event, have someone else do sign-ups so you are free to engage with the guests.

Many settings, particularly newer ones who need to build occupancy quickly, or who have occupancy levels that are too low, have used this method successfully to bring in new families, but there is one word of caution.

If the family commits to taking a place at some point in the distant future (say six months or more) it's important that you take a sensible, non-refundable deposit should they change their minds, or change their committed days and hours. This is critical if you are going to hold a place open, as otherwise, you could sell it to someone else.

Don't forget the key to a significantly successful setting is as close to 100% occupancy as possible.

GOOGLE BUSINESS

Ensuring that your setting is easily found on *Google* is another critical part of lead generation. *Google Business* allows you to add a wealth of information to *Google* to assist users in finding you.

More importantly, though, it provides users with a list of local businesses which are relevant to their search. You will have seen this many times, but you may not know how it works. When you search for a nursery, or even a dentist or plumber, *Google* automatically brings up a page of local providers, displayed on a map of the local area.

Search your local town name plus either the word nursery, pre-school or child minder and see what comes up. For some providers, nothing will come up. And I'll bet for the vast majority of providers what does come-up is an incomplete profile, with no reviews.

It's the *Google* reviews that we need to focus on.

So first of all, you need to register as a business on *Google* and added to *Google Business.*

The good news is this process is relatively easy, but if you don't fancy the task your website provider can do it for you.

If you do want to do it yourself, just search for *Google My Business*, move to the *Google My Business* page, and click the *Start Now* button.

You will need to log into *Google* and navigate to a page called *Add my business*. If you're an existing setting, it's quite likely that your business will appear as you type in the name, at which point you just select the correct company. If not, *Google* will ask you to enter the details of your setting.

Once done, *Google* asks you to verify that you are authorised to add and amend the listing. This either involves *Google* calling you and giving you a verification code or sending one in the post to you. Either way, once you have that code, you can progress to adding information to your *Google* business account.

Within the *Google* account for your business, you can add lots of pertinent information, such an opening hours, and a few paragraphs about what makes your setting special. You can also add photos and images that reflect the calibre of your setting.

All this is really good news for boosting your online profile, and it's free! What more could you ask?

Well actually, *Google* very kindly provides a whole lot more, and unfortunately very few childcare providers are using it!

Google allows parents to write a review of your setting within *Google Business*.

Do you know and use *Trip Advisor* for hotels? Well, *Google* provides the same service for any local business.

So, once your *Google Business* page is set up, go back to those parents who have provided a testimonial and persuade them to add the same testimonial to your *Google Business* page.

Just think, if very few childcare providers are using this facility in your locality and suddenly when a parent searches for childcare in your local region, one provider (yours) comes up with ten reviews! Prospective parents are, undoubtedly, going to give you a call!

BING

And once you have completed the *Google Business* page you need to do exactly the same for the search engine *Bing*.

In this case, it's called *Bing* places, and can be found at *bingplaces.com*

You have the same opportunities to affect search engine results here as you do in *Google Business,* so make sure to register your setting, add photos and unique selling points and get parents to provide testimonials.

FACEBOOK

I could write a whole book about using *Facebook* for childcare, but this will just have to wait for another day.

The short and easy advice for you now is you need to have a *Facebook* page for your business and to update it regularly.

There are two types of *Facebook* pages, a personal page, and a business page. You will almost certainly have a *Facebook* personal page, and you absolutely know how to use it. A *Facebook* business page, however, is slightly different. Before we go into this, please don't use your personal page for your business.

These pages need to be kept separate. No matter how careful you are, there will always be some cheeky friend who will upload a picture of you that is not suitable for your customers. If it hasn't happened to you yet, it will!

So, no matter what, never allow your personal page to be used for business.

What's a business *Facebook* page? A *Facebook* business page is designed as a communication page for customers. It's often used for sales and marketing but really comes to the fore as a means of communicating with existing parents. It's also a brilliant way of promoting your services to the *Facebook* friends of your existing parents, every time they 'like' something that you have posted. And don't forget, every time one of your parents *Likes* a posting on your *Facebook* page, it's automatically added to the feed of all of their friends. That's instant promotion for your setting, to lots of other local families, every time you post something interesting. An instant win!

Setting up a *Facebook* business page is easy, and most importantly, it's free. So if you haven't got one, or aren't using yours, now is the time to action this effective marketing tool.

Using your existing personal *Facebook* profile login to *Facebook*. Then navigate to *www.facebook.com/pages*

In the top right-hand corner, you will see a button called *Create Page*. Simply click it.

This opens up a new screen with six different types of organisation options. Select *Local Business or Place* and scroll down to the *Choose a Category* menu to *Education*.

The rest of this section is very obvious to complete, but before you enter your setting's name, just give some thought to consistency with how else you use your brand name in printed materials and on the web. Whatever you use here should be the same as you use everywhere else. So, if you're *London Road Nursery* don't suddenly be *London Rd Nursery* here, keep it the same.

You next have to enter vital information about your setting.

Within *Categories* add the type of setting you represent.

It's important here to use as many ways of describing your setting as possible. So, rather than saying just nursery, add *Children's nursery, Day Care, Childcare, Early Years,* and *nursery.* This will cover the five main keywords for our sector.

Then add a few sentences about your setting.

Make sure you include your WHY and your *USPs.*

If you have an *Outstanding Ofsted* grade, shout about it! If you have owned the setting for 12 years, tell people. Just be careful though to double-check the spelling here, as a mistake will look really bad.

Add your website address in the relevant box, and finally, bearing in mind the advice about names, add a name for your *Facebook* web address. This address will read *www.facebook.com/LondonRoadNursery.*

Click the *Next* button and add an image. Click *Next* and add the page to your *Favourites* and lastly skip the section on *Facebook* advertising.

You will then land on your sparkly new *Facebook* page specifically for your setting. Invite as many friends and colleagues to join you there as you can.

If they *Like* the page they will receive updates on their *Facebook* feed every time you upload something so go back to your enrolment systems and ensure that you specifically tell new parents that your setting is on *Facebook* and they can follow what happens simply by liking your page.

Now, if all that sounds a bit frivolous, it's not!

Once you start to regularly post images and content to your page, parents will start to *Like* and share what you post. As they do this, so it will be broadcast to their *Facebook* networks, many of whom will be local families and so you start to spread the word about how brilliant your setting is.

Remember that referrals from customers are the highest value lead, and that your existing customers are your secret sales force.

On *Facebook* your customers are unknowingly referring and therefore selling your service.

Remember, nothing beats a testimonial from an existing parent. In the case of *Facebook*, parents won't even know they are endorsing your business, they'll simply think about the wonderful time their children are having at your setting!

This free service will create loads of free endorsements. All you have to do is keep posting content.

So what content should you post?

- Post interesting Childcare news.
- Engage with the local community by promoting local events and local companies and other organisations.
- Add photos and video where you can.
- Actively engage your audience.

Of course, before you add any photos of children to the internet, it is essential to ensure that you have parents' permission, and also ensure that you do not name the children.

How frequently should you post? Daily is ideal.

Lastly, do not make the mistake of making your *Facebook* page *sales-y*. This should be a fun and supportive service for parents. The fact that it will drive enquiries, via shares and likes, is just an amazing added bonus. Make sure your parents know about your page. Make sure you are social.

BRANDING

Branding is how a business is positioned within its locality. It isn't just your logo or your imagery, rather it's the sum of all of the ways you interact with the community, from the way you answer the phone through to how your staff walk through your community wearing their nursery t-shirts.

A common mistake made by small businesses is the perception they need to act like large commercial brands and simply place their logo in prominent places like *Coca-Cola* or *Visa*. Big companies do this so their brands are front of mind at all times.

Most small businesses don't have the money to invest in this sort of branding. That said, some successful settings do use local radio advertising to create a brand within their community, and those that do are convinced it adds value.

What is effective irrespective of the size of the setting is ensuring the brand is used consistently. So on every document, every advert, every sign, every time the phone is answered, the same *Name* is used in the same format. As with the previous example, if you are *London Road Nursery*, don't sometimes be *London Rd Nursery*, or *London Road Childcare*.

Fix your name and imagery, and keep using it in the exact same format.

Finally, I want to highlight an easy mistake I've seen a small chain of nurseries make. This group invested in a marketing agency to create a really good image for their brand.

They then invested in sponsoring many of the roundabouts in their local area. The mistake though, is the brand name, does not include the word nursery, or any image to imply what this company does.

So there are these beautiful signs on loads of roundabouts proudly proclaiming this company's name. If you know of them, it will work perfectly, if you don't it will have no effect whatsoever, as there is no means to know what it is about. Not even a web address.

CONCLUSION

The most successful settings, have thought carefully about their marketing and have made it their top priority until the setting is full.

They have carefully considered their *USPs* and ensure they are conveyed within their marketing messages.

They understand the monetary value of a customer and how much a lead is truly worth. Armed with that knowledge they are able to determine how much they are willing to spend to attract a new customer. They also understand how an enquiry makes its way through the marketing funnel so they can optimise it and identify where leakages occur.

Successful settings understand the real value of testimonials, especially digital testimonials. They have a structured mechanism to ensure there is a steady, consistent stream of testimonials to promote their business.

They ensure testimonials show on local searches to give free kudos with local families and they use *Facebook* as an effective, free referral and advertising mechanism.

KEY POINTS

1. **Ensure that you measure your capacity revenue wastage** in monetary terms. Successful settings do this to highlight how important it is to ensure the setting is full, and to give them a value for their wasted capacity. Focusing on this single measure has a massively positive impact on the business. *Chapter 11* talks about what you should measure within your setting. For now it's worth knowing that everything measured improves. Why? Because you focus on it. Make sure you measure your capacity revenue wastage.

2. **Ensure your website is mobile responsive and contains *Calls To Action*.** You must have a website that generates leads to achieve full occupancy. If your website fails to generate leads, get a better website provider quickly.

3. **Build and Use a 'List' to supplement your website,** remembering that it typically takes five to 14 *touches* before a prospect is ready to engage.

4. **Use written testimonials and video testimonials** on your website and within your outbound email marketing, as methods of reassuring prospect families of the quality of your education.

5. **Use referrals as a primary source of lead generation. Referred customers are almost always pre-sold by someone else.** These are your strongest, most valuable leads. Always treat them like gold dust and nurture them until they become customers.

6. **Ensure you are registered on *Google local* and *Bing*** with useful information and testimonials.

7. **Use *Facebook* to your advantage.**

Al's Rant

I am becoming increasingly concerned about how many unscrupulous companies are selling nursery websites that are simply not fit-for-purpose. They end up being online brochures, which attract little traffic and generate very few leads. This may have been OK in the early noughties, but today it's simply ripping off nursery owners.

Be very wary of website providers who say they specialise in our sector when in fact they build for all sectors. Ensure that you engage a website company that will ensure your website generates leads.

Later in this book, I talk about the need to save costs. This is one area where you shouldn't.

Remember the value of a lead! You need a quality website that consistently brings in quality leads.

Chapter 4:
Converting Prospects To Customers

"Nothing happens until somebody sells something."
Elmer Letterman

The *Parenta National Childcare Survey* confirmed that the average occupancy throughout the sector was 74%. And yet there are nurseries who are consistently full and have waiting lists. They do this by ensuring that once prospective parents have enquired their engagement and conversion processes are absolutely perfect.

Key Finding
The most successful settings focus a huge amount of energy and attention into ensuring that each show round is as effective as possible.

They ensure the whole process is systematised and that every interaction is documented. They measure conversion rates by staff member to identify where further training is needed.

- Do you have a systematised method for converting prospects to customers?
- Do you measure your conversion rate for each staff member?

- Are you confident the way every member of staff deals with enquiries is consistent?
- Are your *show-rounds* as effective as they can be at converting prospects?

PROSPECT VISITS

A couple of years ago, my wife and I were invited to visit to a small chain of nurseries as prospective parents. We were looking to find a place for our, then, two-year-old son. This was their sixth setting which had been open for about eight months.

The appointment was pre-arranged and we arrived at the agreed time. After struggling to get through the front door, we were shown by a receptionist into a waiting room.

The waiting room was set-up well, with couches, folders of policies and procedures, and a really bright and cheery collage of photos of the children at play. On the shelf were pamphlet holders containing the prospectus, another with an application form and a third with the price list.

All in all, you could clearly see that the intention was to create a positive, warm experience for parents to wait.

Only the execution wasn't quite right.

There were several ceiling tiles missing, and the room was clearly being used as a temporary store space, with boxes of flat-pack furniture leaning against one wall and boxes of consumables stacked in front of the photo display. Worst of all, the floor was littered with crisps, most of them trodden in. With a busy day of show rounds, you can see how that had happened, but why weren't they cleared up?

We were offered teas and coffees and told the deputy manager would be with us shortly. She arrived a few minutes later and showed us around the setting. The tour was good and very informative though none of the staff greeted us or said hello. We concluded in the outside play area.

As we wrapped up though things got worse. There was no attempt whatsoever to engage with us about what we were looking for. Did we want full time or a few mornings? The setting doesn't know, as they didn't ask. They didn't even ask for our contact details.

Neither did they try to close the sale or do anything at all to try to sell their service. It was simply, 'Thank you for your visit, let us know if you'd like more information'. Worse still, there was no follow up whatsoever.

Contrast this with a client I work with in the South East.

This is a chain of two, and we were asked to look at the second setting. As before, the appointment was pre-arranged.

This time, we were greeted at the door by the manager, and shown into a clean, smart room, again with sofas where we were offered tea and were asked about our needs and what we were looking for.

We then had an age-appropriate tour of the setting which was informative. Importantly, the manager used the name of our child throughout the tour ("This is where Jake will be starting his day....") and every member of staff we met acknowledged us (Jake included).

We were then taken back to the reception room where the manager talked us through the options, including available days and Free Entitlement.

She also explained the settings entry requirements which included an administration fee and deposit. She explained clearly why a deposit was required and when it would be returned, and also explained the billing process and how important it was, as a small business, that they were paid on time.

She cleverly spun all of the negatives associated with deposits and late fees into positives.

She then went on to ask us which days we'd like Jake to attend (an assumptive close in selling terms).

The process was so good, so smooth and so positive that if we had lived in that area we would have signed-up on the spot.

The point of this story is too many settings are failing at getting the conversion process right. A systematised tour with a structured sales pitch at the end is easy to implement.

GETTING THE CONVERSION PROCESS RIGHT

These two stories highlight the importance of ensuring that all interactions with prospects are perfect.

The next issue is ensuring that the interactions of prospects with every member of your staff is perfect.

And I don't use the word perfect lightly. If a customer has picked up the phone to engage with you, it's critical that whoever deals with the enquiry does so in a structured and competent manner. It's too easy to blow this key part of your customer acquisition model.

To make this work, you need two specific pitches. One for the telephone conversation and another for the show round. You also need to ensure that the show around is a structured, logical, professional, friendly and above all, happy experience.

All large companies invest in sales pitches. This is true for all the brands that you know and love, from *Virgin* to *BMW*, from *Ferrari* to *Apple*. The big brands know that structured conversations work, whereas informal *chit-chat* doesn't. Your customer acquisition model needs structured sales scripts to ensure that this part of the process is smooth and inspires confidence.

THE TELEPHONE PITCH

Ambitious businesses work hard on achieving the perfect business pitch. In your line of work, it's imperative you have a structured pitch or script so that whoever deals with an enquiry does so in a professional manner. This is so important. Many nurseries, pre-schools, and childminders have a huge hole in their enquiry funnel due to this very weakness. Why? Because answering the phone is not seen as important.

Let's go back to basics. We have learned that an enquiry is worth up to £50,000 to you, *and* most enquiries come via the telephone. So answering the phone to prospective parents is a *critical* part of your enquiry funnel and one that you absolutely *must* get right. Its worth up to £50,000!

Unfortunately, my experience here suggests two common problems:

- The person answering the phone is unable to deal with the enquiry and has to get their manager to call them back.
- The person answering the phone tries their best to deal with the enquiry but simply isn't effective.

There is a third problem, but thankfully this occurs less these days, but it does still happen.

- The person answering the phone just doesn't care!

In all of the above cases, you leave your prospect with a poor experience of your business, which is a luxury few providers can afford. Worse still, with the callback scenario it's not uncommon for calls to be forgotten, or for the call to be returned at a time which is really inconvenient to your prospect. How would you feel in this scenario? Happy to send *your* child there?

It is the experience on the call, and during the show round that makes the most significant impact on your income, so you cannot afford anything less than perfection.

You will need to spend time and effort crafting your pitch, and you should base it on your experience of dealing with the specific questions parents ask, whilst considering how you will convey your WHY and your *USPs*. Specific skills are needed to ensure you are able to convert the enquirer into someone who is motivated to take a tour of your facilities. Think through all the potential objections, determine answers and if necessary role play. You *have* to get this right.

If you are simply asked about the price at this point, you've got it wrong!!

As you craft your pitch or script, be very clear about the outcome you need.

The outcome of your telephone pitch is to book an appointment with the prospects so they come to see your setting and get an experience of how you and your team work. It is not, I repeat, not, to get prospects to sign up there and then. This is frequently forgotten.

Make sure you have a system by your phone, so you can immediately and confidently make the booking. There is nothing worse than a bumbling response whilst you find your calendar and slowly work out when you have space to see a prospect.

Ensure you send a letter or email or a text to the parents confirming their appointment.

This has two critical objectives. One, it ensures that the parents have a written note of the appointment; and secondly, it confirms that your operation is professional.

One last thing: demeanour is easily recognised on the phone. If the person answering is stressed or having a bad day, the caller is likely to sense it. Worse still are those staff who are bored, miserable or disengaged: we all know phone responses like this.

Ensure that staff dealing with enquiries not only understand what to say but also how to say it, and how to sound. Teach them to smile whilst they talk. Even on the phone, it makes such a difference!

THE IMPORTANCE OF BEING CUSTOMER FOCUSED

A friend has been asking my advice about local nurseries as she wants to move her little boy of three from his current setting. Not that there's anything wrong with the current one – indeed, she was keen to keep telling me how good it was but she felt her son would be better prepared for primary school if he attended a bigger setting.

I gave her some suggestions and off she went to get in contact. She did her research. She looked at the websites of all the settings I suggested, and based on her research, had a short list and a clear favourite.

Now, given that the average occupancy for settings is 74%, you'd think this lady and her son would be a prime candidate for all the settings. You'd think they'd be desperate to engage her and welcome her little boy.

But that's not what happened! The lady rang three nurseries to organise a time to visit - preferably on the day she and her partner had off work.

When she called her preferred setting the phone rang for ages. Eventually an answer phone kicked in and she left a message saying she was interested in a viewing. Over 24 hours later she didn't have a response.

The other two were not much better. One said only the manager could help and she would call back. The other could only offer a viewing at an inconvenient time.

Let's just take a minute to think about this! Let's assume average fees for a full-time place at a nursery are £1,000 per month and the average occupancy for all three nurseries is 74%.

The child is three and so has at least another year to go until he starts school. So, it's pretty likely that the *opportunity* is for the child to be with the setting for 12 months on a full-time basis. So that's £1,000 x 12 = £12,000.

The cost of adding another child for the year for the setting owner is almost nothing. The setting is staffed, they are below ratio and they have excess capacity. The only real additional cost is the cost of food.

Let's say that's £2.50 per day. So the *cost* of having this extra child is £2.50 x 5 x 52 = £650.

So, the top line revenue for the setting is £12,000 and the only addition cost for having the child at the setting is £650.

This means that an extra £12,000 – £650 = £11,350 would fall to the bottom line (net profit line), simply for taking this child. And imagine if the child was a baby and would be with the nursery for 4.5 years (£11,350 x 4.5 = £51,075 of extra revenue!)

The point here is that by *not* dealing with the enquiry properly, all three settings missed out on over £11,000 in net profit <u>this year</u>.

When you put it this way, you suddenly realise that it's simply bad business to not have your sales systems properly optimised. This means ensuring that the phone is answered quickly with someone who can deal with the enquiry promptly, adequately and professionally. Someone who can take the booking for the show round and offer times that suit the parent.

Again and again, I see settings offering the most amazing childcare, but failing to capitalise on their potential by not optimising their sales and marketing channels.

What's worse is they spend significant sums of money on marketing their setting with websites and listings on online childcare directories, on banners and local media, and then waste the enquiry by failing to ensure the phone is answered properly.

If your occupancy is anything like the 74% average, focusing your attention on the process of bringing new parents into your setting must be your priority as this will have the biggest impact on improving your profitability.

THE SHOW-ROUND

As you already know, the show round is another critical element of improving your occupancy.

If you treat it lightly, you'll not get the levels of occupancy you need to improve your financial results.

The most successful settings think through, in advance, how their show-rounds will work. They plan the agenda of the show-round, how long they'll spend with parents on a one-to-one, how they'll navigate the building and for how long, and how they'll deal with the questions.

Importantly, they consider how they convey and re-enforce their WHY.

So, back to you. You'll need an introductory pitch, which should last no more than a few minutes.

Don't forget, whilst you are probably calm and relaxed, the parents in front of you are likely to be nervous about the prospect of leaving their child.

There are several key elements to a pitch. At the risk of sounding patronising it's worth going back to basics.

Firstly, find somewhere comfortable to talk to your prospects. A busy hallway with pushchairs, wet coats and wellies is not the place.

Ideally, you need a room with a comfy sofa, but I realise finding this space can be difficult. Nonetheless, the more conducive the space for a conversation with parents, the more they'll relax and the easier the pitch will flow.

Make sure your values are clearly displayed on the wall and there are testimonials to hand.

Secondly, make sure you introduce yourself and your position slowly and clearly. Not everyone is called *Jane Smith*, and if your name is in anyway unusual, ensure that the parents actually hear it. What would be more embarrassing for parents than to have to keep asking your name?

Thirdly, make sure you tell them something comforting about your professional experience. You are the one with the experience, knowledge and certificates on the wall to prove it. So make sure you explain why you are suitably qualified to look after their children.

Next, explain clearly, why your vision of childcare is different. Ensure you talk about your WHY and explain your *USPs*. Make sure you promote your values and explain why they are so important to you and your staff.

Fourthly, ask and understand what they are seeking. Once you have this information, adapt your pitch to ensure you address the issues they are looking for. Highlight and reinforce.

As you start the tour, ensure that your staff are well prepared. I will elaborate in a subsequent chapter, but be sure staff are smartly dressed, say hello to your prospects and look them in the eye. Don't underestimate how important this is.

As the tour completes, ideally, return to the room, close the sale and close the meeting. Either way, make sure you have their contact information, and you clearly understand what sessions they are looking for. Don't forget, you'll be adding their names to your list so you can continue to engage with them as they think through their decision. It's critical that you have the correct spelling of their names, and their child's name, particularly taking into account the child's known name, as well as their real name.

ASK FOR THE BUSINESS

Remember my friend who was looking for new childcare for her three-year-old son? She wanted a specific time slot to be shown around but few of the settings she contacted were able to accommodate her request.

So rather than seeing the three nurseries I suggested, she actually visited five.

She told me the merits of each and that she had decided on the right one for her child.

I was interested in how she made the final decision. She chose the *only* setting out of five that followed up on her show-round! That's right, only one out of five settings followed up on a show-round!

I regularly talk to owners about their process for engaging with new parents, and the critical importance of ensuring their sales and marketing channels are optimised so enquiries from prospective parents actually become new parents.

The most successful nurseries I work with have this process *fully* documented and ensure that every interaction with prospective parents is standardised and practised. This process includes a follow-up letter and phone call after every show-round.

This is essential if your occupancy is anything below 90%, as you have to focus on getting your setting full. This means optimising your conversion process (that is, converting enquiring parents into paying parents) as well as your marketing system. There is little point in spending money on adverts and websites if your conversion process is ineffective.

There are two further things that successful nurseries do. *Many of them simply ask for the child to come to that setting!*

Can you imagine going to any other sales environment where you get a tour of the service and not being asked for your business?

Try going to a car showroom or to see a kitchen showroom. Now, before you say they are different, I know that! But the conversion process is the same. It's a prospect being converted into a customer. Simply, why shouldn't you ask for the business?

The second thing the successful settings do is offer a substantial free period, such as the first month, or the first two weeks.

And I'm not talking about taster sessions or settling-in sessions; I'm talking about a genuinely *free trial* of your service.

When I've talked about this with some owners they often recoil in horror! "I can't afford that!" is the first thing they say. But that's rarely true. In fact, this gesture usually costs you very little or nothing and gains you a loyal customer who may be with you for several years paying you tens of thousands of pounds.

Let's assume that you charge £1,000 per month for a full-time session, you have excess capacity and you are below ratio. And let's assume that it costs you £2 per day for food and nappies etc. Finally, for the sake of simplicity let's assume it's a 20-day month, and that you are currently about 70% full.

Your premises costs, and your facilities costs (light, heat, water, rates) you have to pay already and so we can ignore them for this trial for this child. Likewise, staff costs are already covered. Thus, the only *real additional cost* for this child, over and above what you would have to pay anyway, is £2 food etc x 20 days = £40. That's it.

To offer a completely free place to a new child for one month will cost you £40. You could even say to the prospective parent that you offer a free first month; they just have to pay for lunches at £2.50 per day. In this case, you actually have a contribution of £10 for this month.

And if the child is settled in your nursery after the first month, what's the likelihood of them being moved after the free trial? Pretty low, I think!

And so next month, you'd get an extra £1,000 flowing into the business, immediately impacting your net profit line.

The alternative is, you *might* get the customer, or they *might* go somewhere else. Better to stack the odds in your favour.

STAFF INTERACTION

My youngest son is due to start school in six months time. And so my wife and I went to see two local schools.

At the first school, we were greeted by the headmaster. He shook our hands, welcomed us to the school, and then bent down and talked to our son. Once all the visiting parents were assembled, he gave a short speech about the values of the school and what they were trying to achieve and then sent us off on a tour with a couple of the older children.

As we walked into every classroom, the teacher stopped, looked us in the eye, welcomed us in, and explained what they were doing that day. Most (but not all) came over and shook hands.

At every juncture of the visit we were made to feel welcome, that we were not intruding and every member of staff wanted to explain what they were doing. They really showed they cared.

In contrast, at the second school, all the visiting parents were forced to queue up outside. It was bitterly cold so not a great start. We met the Head as she was having a row with another parent about bringing in their pushchair!

Eventually, we were ushered into the main hall where the Head gave a speech. She didn't introduce herself. She didn't welcome us. She just launched into a spiel about how oversubscribed the school was and how we'd be *lucky* to get a place if our child didn't already have siblings at the school, or we didn't live with 0.8 of a mile!

It got worse.

As before, a couple of the older children showed us round. They were delightful and wanted to show *their* school in the best way possible. As we went from classroom to classroom, though, not a single teacher acknowledged our existence. No hellos, no welcome. Not even looking up and acknowledging us. The experience was horrible.

And so you can guess which of the two schools our son will be going to.

I relay this story to highlight how fundamentally important it is that your staff *engage* with prospective parents, as well as the person doing the show round. However, having walked through so many nurseries, I can tell you that as a rule, staff *don't* engage with people being shown around.

They should! It makes all the difference!

PROSPECT NURTURING

So, you've shown prospects around your setting and given them a great impression of you, your staff and your service.

What next? Well, in so many of the settings, the *what next* is nothing.

Nothing!

It's just a wait and see if the parents come back to book a place.

If you're 100% full, then this strategy is probably OK. If not, you need a lead nurturing campaign.

It's easier to explain what a lead nurturing campaign is not, before we talk about what it is.

Lead nurturing *is not:*

- Sending out an e-newsletter on a semi-regular basis.
- Randomly calling parents every six weeks to see if they are ready for their child to attend your school.
- Blasting your entire email database with a new idea.
- Offering content that promotes your setting but doesn't take into account the parent's position in the purchase cycle and their readiness to buy.

Lead nurturing is a system where you provide relevant content in a systematised way to encourage your prospects to place their child with you *when they are ready.*

The technical explanation of a lead nurturing campaign is the process of building relationships with qualified prospects regardless of their timing to buy, with the goal of earning their business when they are ready. Building a relationship with a prospect is the same as with any long-term relationship — you can't force someone to commit (to a purchase, in this case) — but you also cannot afford to lose individuals because their willingness to buy doesn't match your readiness to sell.

Lead nurturing is a system of contact, usually after the customer has visited your setting, but before they have signed a contract, that encourages parents to agree eventually to send their child to you.

The system may involve multiple media.

For instance, without fail, you should post a letter to the parents thanking them for their time, offering the Child - (known name, not first name) a place and confirming what to do next.

Beyond that, there should be a series of three to six contacts, either via email or telephone.

With these contacts, further convey the advantages of your setting, without being overly pushy. It should be short and to the point.

Don't forget the purpose here is to get your prospects to become clients. Remember, they have probably had a tour of other settings too, so it's important to convince your prospects that you care more about their custom, so make your emails personal, but not pushy. It's important you put your prospects interests ahead of your own.

The sequence should be something like this:

Day 1: *Formal letter* addressed to the parents at home, thanking them for their time, and offering a place to their child [known name]. Importantly, if the parents are separated, make sure it goes to both homes; you don't want to alienate one of the parents.

Day 3 or 4: *Telephone call* to one of the parents to gather feedback –making sure that you prepare what you are going to say for any of the following scenarios:

- (Most likely:- Voice mail)
- "We're still thinking about it."
- "We've gone somewhere else."
- "Yes, we'd like a place."

For each of these responses, make sure there is a pre-determined script and action plan.

Day 5: Email.

Day 7 or 8: Email.

Day 10: Email.

You may discover an optimum sequence for your setting that combines the elements of email, phone call, direct mail and visit.

CONCLUSION

Increasing your conversion rates is one of the most important, and one of the cheapest ways of increasing your occupancy. It involves no real expense, just the time to create a systematised mechanism.

The more successful settings have recognised this and ensure that all processes within the Customer acquisition system are robust and have been practised repeatedly. They also measure the conversion rate of each person who undertakes show rounds so that skills can be transferred.

Successful settings also stack the odds in their favour by taking advantage of their fixed costs to offer extended, quality, trial places for new children.

Successful settings understand that conducting a show round, without a pre-determined script and without prospectuses and contracts are, in fact, just a cosy chat.

They emulate successful sales organisations and ensure that all the elements are in place to ask for the sale at the time of the show-round and for the parent to complete their contract there and then.

KEY POINTS

1. Ensure your setting has thoroughly worked out the whole process for show rounds.

- Prospects should ideally be shown into a specific room to discuss enrolling their children.
- The whole show-round process should be fully documented and practised repeatedly until it is a slick operation.
- Ensure that all relevant sales materials are available to close the sale as the show round concludes.

- Always try to close the sale at the time.
- Always ensure that you have a full and comprehensive follow-up process.
- Always ensure you have captured the parent's details, the name of the child and mechanisms to stay in touch.

2. Ensure telephone pitches are properly scripted and that every member of staff is capable of dealing with the enquiry professionally.

- Ensure answering the phone is treated as a key part of the conversion process.
- Ensure everyone who answers the phone is well trained to answer prospects questions and to steer them to a show round.

3. Measure the conversion rate of every member of staff who undertakes show-rounds. Use discrepancies amongst staff to provide further training.

4. Make sure all staff acknowledge and greet prospects. No excuses. The impact of a warm welcome *and* a fond farewell cannot be emphasised enough.

Al's Rant

There are significant opportunities for settings who are struggling to increase their occupancy through improving their conversion processes. And best of all, it's completely free.

We live in an age where most of the younger generation are permanently glued to their smartphones. Why then is the process of answering the phone treated so poorly?

After interacting with a website, the first real contact between a prospect and the setting is via the telephone.

It needs to be right!

Chapter 5: Customer Engagement

"We see our customers as invited guests to a party, and we are the hosts. It's our job every day to make every important aspect of the customer experience a little bit better".
Jeff Bezos, CEO, Amazon.com

Within the *Parenta National Childcare Survey, Customer Engagement* was the one element where Childcare providers felt they had things pretty right. In fact, 100% of our respondents felt they had good engagement strategies in place and 63% undertook an annual parent survey. Could it be even better?

Key Finding
Most settings feel they get the Customer Engagement part of their business right. Successful settings go further, though. Successful settings offer extended levels of customer service which make the parents say *WOW!* They understand the impact of creating *WOW!* customer service, not only on their current customers but also on future customers.

- Do you provide *WOW!* customer service in your setting?
- Are all of your staff fully engaged with all existing parents?
- Do all of your staff greet all of your customers by name? Even those who only collect once a week?

THE IMPORTANCE OF CUSTOMER ENGAGEMENT

In my local town, there are two restaurants that opened at about the same time two years ago. One is serving French food and the other Italian. They are in the same part of town and have about the same number of covers. And yet the French one is always full and the Italian never has more than a hand-full of customers. In fact, the French restaurant is currently booking tables for Friday and Saturday nights four to five months in advance.

When you enter the French restaurant you are immediately greeted warmly and shown to your table.

During the meal, without exception, even on the busiest nights, the owner comes over and asks you personally how everything was with your meal. And I don't mean the *Is everything OK* style of asking that you get in all the chain restaurants. I mean a genuine interest in your experience. At the end of every meal, the staff also offer a complimentary brandy.

Everything about this restaurant says that they care. The service is brilliant in every respect. In fact, it's *WOW!* Everybody recommends it to friends and it's become number one on *TripAdvisor*.

Contrast this with the Italian place.

You walk in and wait around for someone to greet you. They show you to a table, but there's no enthusiasm, it's just *'… here you go.'*

When the meal arrives it is plonked in front of you. You can never catch the waiter's eye to order more drink or the bill, and when you do eventually get the bill there's no warmth. It's just perfunctory.

The sad thing about this restaurant is the food is reasonably good. But the service is ordinary and therefore the 'experience' is poor. People do not recommend it.

Back in *Chapter 3*, we identified that over 60% of enquiries for new business for child carers come from word of mouth. This clearly proves, just like the two restaurants, that your existing customers are the biggest advocates of your business, and drive more new enquiries than any other source.

Remember also, that a new full-time customer is potentially worth up to £50,000.

These two facts make it essential your existing customers are actively talking positively about the service you provide.

Indeed, your customers should be your greatest marketing asset. They offer the easiest opportunity for increased revenues from upselling, and the best opportunity to bring new customers to your door via direct recommendations and testimonials.

Now, I'm sure that in the vast majority of cases, your customers are content with the service you provide. If they weren't, they'd leave your setting and move their child.

But there is a difference between customers who are content and those who think your service is so amazing that they'll shout about how wonderful it is to all of their friends.

Indeed, content customers often feel that service can be better. They don't move because the *cost* of moving is too great – in the case of childcare, often not in a monetary sense but in an emotional sense.

Successful settings have figured out how to move their standard of service up to the ladder from *Good*, past *Great* and into *WOW!*

Providing *WOW!* service constantly takes effort. It means you will need to take your staff on a journey to where every customer interaction is planned and perfected, and where ensuring the customer experience (the customer that pays the bills and recommends you to their friends) is exceptional, as well as the experience of the child.

WOW! service has incredible value to you. It sets you apart from your competitors, it gets you full quicker, and most importantly, it allows you to become more profitable, as it allows you to increase your prices.

WOW! service also changes the perception of your business

within your community. It allows you to compete against the shiny new building up the road by giving you an unfair advantage. *WOW!* takes time to get right, and takes a while to ingrain with your staff and your systems, but once implemented sets you apart from your competitors.

Once you achieve a reputation for *WOW!* it will remain in your community for a long time.

WOW! SERVICE

Within any service environment, there is a ladder assessing the standard of service. It starts at no-service and progresses upwards as follows:

- No service.
- Bad/Poor service.
- Average service.
- Expected anyway.
- Not anticipated.
- *WOW!*

Does your setting provide *WOW!* service? Or is it more of the expected anyway type of service?

In his brilliant book *Give Your Guest a WOW!*, Adam Hamadache describes a *WOW!* as something that your customers don't expect. He says if that *something* comes up as a topic of conversation at a dinner party, then you have clearly delivered a *WOW!* moment.

I was recently a recipient of *WOW!* service and was so impressed, I talked about it on my personal *Facebook* page, the modern equivalent of talking about it at a dinner party!

I visited a client who runs a chain of nurseries in Dubai and I took the opportunity to add extra days to see the city with my wife.

At breakfast in our hotel, a hostess greeted me by name and asked about our plans for the day. I explained we planned to relax by the pool before flying home the next day.

As we left the lounge, we were presented with the following card, signed by all the staff, along with a bag containing vitamin waters, juices, soft drinks and sun creams. Now, that's *WOW!* service. They didn't need to, but they took the time to make sure our experience was something special.

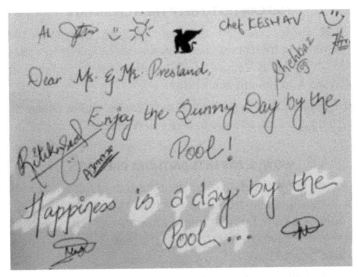

So, a *WOW!* is an element of service that adds value to your customers. It is something that sets you apart and makes your customers talk about you.

Here are some examples of *WOWs*. I'm sure you can think of many more.

WOW! 1: TEXT PARENTS ABOUT TRAFFIC PROBLEMS IN THE AREA

For parents who drive to your setting where there is a traffic issue in your immediate area, it would be easy for you to text all your parents as soon as you hear about it to give them fair warning.

Remember to keep the text friendly, we don't want it to be seen as trying to ensure parents aren't late, you simply want to let them know.

"Just wanted to let you know that I've heard the M5 is blocked at J6. Hope it's not too bad, see you when you get here. Jill."

WOW! 2: TEXT PARENTS A WEEK IN ADVANCE OF THEIR CHILD'S BIRTHDAY TO SEE IF THERE IS ANYTHING YOU CAN DO TO HELP THEM CELEBRATE

What better way to tell parents that you care than remembering their child's birthday a week before! Noting each child's birthday is a piece of cake with nursery management software! And the impact is huge.

"Hi Susan, Can't believe it's Rosie's 2nd birthday next week. Anything you'd like us to do to help you celebrate?"

WOW! 3: PARENTS BIRTHDAY PRESENTS

Do you know the date of birth of the parents? If you do, why not offer a present from the child for the parent's birthday. It could be a card, but that might interfere with your planning. What about having a stock of small presents (low value) for the child to give to Dad.

Text the other parent the week before.

"Hi Rachel, As it's Rosie's dad's birthday next week, do you want us to organise something for Rosie to give him? We have wrapped chocs at £9.99. Just let me know. Thanks, Jill x"

WOW! 4: CUSTOMER LOYALTY PACKAGES

If children have been with you for a few years how about sending a loyalty bonus to the parents? It doesn't have to cost much, and could be something simple, like a free class at the weekend, to a box of chocs. The *what* doesn't really matter.

The key is acknowledging what a great customer they have been. Guess how many people they'll tell about your caring attitude and brilliant customer service?

WOW! 5: CHILDREN'S BIRTHDAYS

Acknowledge children's birthdays within the reception area. Put up a list of children's birthdays every day. It makes parents feel special, as well as the child.

WOW! 6: CHILDREN'S BIRTHDAYS

Ensure every child leaves the setting with something exciting on their birthday. The cost is very low, and yet again you are seen to care and to go beyond the norm.

WOW! 7: CHILDREN'S BIRTHDAYS

So, it's Bella's birthday today. And her best friend's mum has just arrived at reception and realised that she had forgotten and didn't have anything for her daughter to give to Bella. Hey presto. You have a range of low-value gifts and cards that mum can buy to instantly solve this problem.

WOW! 8: FRESH FRUIT

Keep a bowl of cut fresh fruit in reception for the children to help themselves to as they leave. It creates a positive impression, is definitely something parents will talk about, and is equally valuable to impress prospective parents.

With many of these ideas, there is a small element of cost involved. However these costs are tiny compared with the goodwill from parents, and positive reviews !

And, as long as your management software is flexible, you're going to charge the parents anyway. Just think how valuable these testimonials and recommendations are to you.

Don't forget your current customers are the strongest source of recommendations as they tell their network of friends. If you have your *Facebook* page set-up as discussed in *Chapter 3*, always add an image of each of these *WOWs* so that parents like them, which expands the good impression to their whole friendship group.

STAFF ENGAGEMENT

Staff engagement is also a critical aspect of customer engagement. Smartly dressed, happy staff who look parents in the eye and talk to them are the keys to customer engagement.

Make the personal connection better still by ensuring that your staff know the names of the parents. It's your choice if you want to use their first name, or their last name, but don't under-estimate the power of every member of staff knowing the names of parents, and greeting them every time they walk past. It is so much more professional than being *Maddie's Dad*. (I have never been addressed personally by any of the staff at any of the settings that my children have attended. What a wasted opportunity! Especially given the example of the hotel where they greeted my wife and I as Mr and Mrs Presland at every opportunity and we were only there for four days!

There's an easy way to cheat here to get this right.

On the child's first day, take a snap of both parents. With most nursery management systems, you can add the images directly, which helps you keep track. Explain that it's for security reasons.

Then, print the photos out, and put them up in the staff room, or give small versions to your staff to learn their names (this is what high-end hotels do). It makes such a difference being greeted by name. By the way, this is a wow, not a *WOW!* It's great, it will set you apart from the competition, but isn't it something that your customers should expect from you anyway?

USE IT SYSTEMS

Two years ago, I was seated in a finance class at a conference with lots of delegates. I got talking to the people around the table and we each explained what we did.

As I explained my role within the childcare sector, one of the men described how brilliant the nursery was that his daughter attended.

We got into a conversation and he talked about many factors he liked about the nursery, including the messages sent home. It turns out that as he leaves early in the morning to commute to London, and arrives home late, he rarely gets to see his girls in the nursery setting.

And yet he was excitedly telling me how he receives emails every day from the setting explaining what the girls were doing with photos of them at play. It also included how they were progressing, and what they ate each day.

He found it an amazing way to feel involved with his daughter's progress, even though he was constantly remote.

It turns out the nursery was using *Parenta's* products and given that they are unbranded, he believed they came directly from the nursery itself. It was great to hear he liked the service!

Whether you use *Parenta's* services, or those of any other vendor, modern IT systems have unique ways of extending beyond the boundaries of the setting and into your customer's homes.

Parent portals and smartphone based parent *App*s allow parents to review the key information held within your software system which is a great way to increase engagement with parents and definitely satisfies regulatory requirements to treat parents as partners.

Systems like *Parenta's Daycare* allow parents to view photos and videos of what's happening in the nursery, and EYFS tracking software (such as *Parenta's Footsteps*) will allow your parents to see how their child is progressing.

Whichever element you use, whether it's produced by *Parenta* or other vendors, you extend your offering into your parent's home and increase customer engagement.

PRODUCT EXTENSION

The most successful settings offer extra products and services to both their customer base and their community.

Whilst many providers deliver after school clubs few seem to go beyond this offering. And yet most providers have extensive properties that lie empty at weekends and evenings. What a wasted opportunity!

Shortly, we'll be talking about finance and how to improve that within a setting. And within the finance chapter, I'll say that it is often harder to decrease your costs than it is to increase revenues. This is because your costs are usually pretty fixed. Rent (or mortgage costs), rates etc are what they are, and you're unlikely to be able to change them.

You can increase your revenues, however, *relatively* easily by adding new services to your portfolio.

Don't forget, the cost of renting the building, or paying the mortgage is already sunk, so excluding the variable costs of extra staff, all the additional revenues tend to go straight to the bottom line!

For those of you who don't offer after school clubs, this is an obvious way of extending your relationships with your customers and increasing the revenue per customer.

Beyond this, though, anything that utilises the investment you have in your buildings when you are not using them is advantageous.

One setting I work with opens up every Saturday and Sunday as a play centre for local children. This is an excellent way of further spreading the costs of these assets.

But you can easily go further. Ideas for further uses of your building during evenings and weekends include:

- Birthday parties.
- Music lessons.
- Drama Classes.

- Exercise classes.
- Craft parties.
- Tutoring.
- Fitness lessons.

The clever part of offering these is to get a third party in to develop them and somehow split the revenue. Better still, offer a discount to your current parents – immediately seen then as a benefit of using your facilities, whilst charging the general public at the standard rate.

These opportunities not only change the dynamic of your settings finances (extra revenue – no real extra work, more connection with your existing parents), but it also gets new people through your door.

Now, if these new people like your environment, and see the brilliant testimonials you have on the wall, where do you think they'll recommend to their friends who have just had a new baby? One opportunity leads to the next!

But there are more things you can offer. Let's think about our target audience. In many cases it's busy parents who are working long hours.

Help them!

Engage with local businesses and offer their services through your setting. Of course, you will always expect a cut of the revenue, but it could very easily become a win for you, a win for the parent and a win for the local business.

For instance, one chain of nurseries I've worked with facilitated parent's dry cleaning. Easy to arrange and easy to implement. Massive value to the parents and additional revenue to you.

And don't forget, you can bet which childcare setting that dry cleaner recommends to all those who stop to chat.

CUSTOMER RELATIONSHIP BUILDING

Compared with most small businesses, you are in the very privileged provision of being able to provide a direct relationship with every customer each day. Just think how much most businesses would pay for that opportunity; the ability to greet all of their customer's every day!

The most successful settings I work with recognise that this is a tremendous opportunity and make the time to be available to greet parents and children daily. And I mean greet them and engage with them.

And you could take it a stage further.

What if you hired a gourmet coffee machine and some of those *to-go* cups with the lids on. The coffee and the cup work out to about 50p per drink.

Now let's say mum drops off her child, and as she leaves, you hand her a *branded* cup of coffee. For free.

Yep, for free. You just give her a cup of coffee as she leaves the building.

So, let's work out what that would cost. Say there are 50 children at the setting. And you offer this service only on a Friday. If every single parent took a coffee (they wouldn't, but we'll assume they could). This would cost you £25 (£0.50 x 50).

Now let's say you do that every Friday for a year. That's £25 x 52 = £1,250 per year.

Just think about this for a minute. For £1,250 you can have 50 parents walking around, and arriving at work, every Friday *advertising your setting.*

Oh, and of course, do you think they'll tell their friends about it? And do you think it would enhance client relationships?

Let's look at it another way. If the parent is paying £1,000 per month, that extra loyalty and that branding is costing you just £2 per month or just over 1/5th of 1 percent.

What an investment in client relationships and *WOW!*

Let me give you another example.

A few years ago I was at a nursery as parents started to collect their children at the end of the day. It was summer time and the children were all out in the garden.

It was a large nursery with lots of children.

There were the requisite number of staff on duty, but none of them seemed particularly interested in what was going on.

Some were huddled chatting in the middle whilst others were standing by slides watching the children.

What was bizarre was the way they interacted with the parents as they came to collect their children.

Parents would come into the garden, stop whilst they looked around for their little one, and then go and pick them up.

Some would ask if their child had been OK that day, but the answers were always the same and delivered in a completely bored way.

The parents would then simply leave to return to the main building and collect their child's belongings.

There was no real interaction. The staff made no effort whatsoever to engage with the parents; they seemed far more interested in continuing to chat!

What a wasted opportunity to engage with the parents and to explain how and what the children had been doing all day. Now, I know that many settings get this right, but not all!

CONCLUSION

The most successful settings recognise the importance of customer engagement. They recognise that customer experience challenges the status quo and allows them to offer higher, or even premium prices.

These settings, have implemented *WOW!* systems to ensure that the customer's experience is frequently greater than they expect. In turn, parents also become huge advocates of the settings and the service they receive and it is them who become the marketing advocates.

Successful setting also recognise that IT can play a significant role in enhancing the customer experience. Using parent *Apps* which link to nursery management systems and nursery learning software enhance and further develop your partnership with parents.

KEY POINTS

1. **Customer Engagement enables you to charge higher prices** as parents recognise they receive an enhanced service. Higher prices are the easiest way to increase profitability.

2. **Creating an enhanced customer experience is the cheapest and most effective way of marketing your nursery.** Parents talking to their friends about how good the service is, and how they are surprised by *WOWs* creates the desire for other parents to experience the same.

3. **Use modern IT systems and parent *Apps* to share each child's day** with parents.

4. **Ensure all your staff are fully engaged and talking to parents.** Give them the tools to address every parent by name, including those who pick-up only occasionally.

Al's Rant

Delivering exceptional customer service and customer experiences requires extra thought, but it is, with commitment, relatively easy to implement. But in the majority of businesses in the UK, this seems to be of little priority.

How often have you been in a queue in a shop whilst several members of staff have stood around chatting or stacking shelves? It doesn't have to be this way, and really should never be this way in childcare.

We should be leading from the front and showing how great we can make customer experiences.

CHAPTER 6: COLLECTING FEES

"Turnover is vanity, profit is sanity and cash is reality."
Unknown

The *Parenta National Childcare Survey* revealed some alarming details about the level of bad debt within the sector. The problem is significant with over half of settings saying they have had to write-off bad debt within the last year.

> ### Key Finding
> The most successful settings rarely have to deal with bad debt. They avoid bad-debt and struggling to pay bills by ensuring that their fee collection systems are automated and robust and by ensuring there is no revenue leakage or wastage. Being profitable, they have cash available to ensure that bills are paid on time and are not therefore saddled with having to deal with irate suppliers and the stress of meeting payroll when funds are tight.

- How are you at collecting payments on time?
- Are you having to deal with bad debt on a regular basis?
- Do you have customers who owe you money?
- Do you often find it difficult to pay all of your bills on time, and end up dealing with irate suppliers?

Collecting payments owing is often the most disliked aspect of running a childcare business, and yet it's one of the most important.

WHY IS CASH FLOW A PROBLEM?

Too many childcare providers struggle with cash flow. In the main, this is due to a combination of having poor fee collection procedures, poor profitably and the curse of most childcare providers; simply being too nice!

Collecting the money due to you is the absolute lifeblood of all companies, large and small. Prompt payment controls everything and makes life exceedingly difficult if not pursued robustly. Running out of cash leads to business failure.

The need for robust fee collection systems, therefore, should not be underestimated.

Many years ago, I was with a husband and wife team who ran a small chain of nurseries. They were heavily into branding and created a great image for themselves in the local area. They had also invested in a new modern building for their third setting with some of the most amazing facilities I have seen in any nursery, at that time or since. All of their settings had good regulatory body grades, and on the surface, everything looked rosy. I spent several hours there, and we discussed a huge array of issues. We talked about profitability and whilst their results weren't stellar, they were certainly respectable.

Part way through my visit, though, the wife suddenly burst into tears. It turns out, that whilst everything looked great on the surface, they had absolutely no cash, they were really struggling to make payroll each month and were behind with paying tax and many suppliers to the extent that they had used their personal credit cards to cover payments and just had nowhere left to turn.

So we pulled their *aged debt report* from their nursery management system and immediately found the answer to the issue. They simply weren't focusing enough attention on collecting their fees.

Just as we were talking, though, a family walked past the window and the wife said: "Just look at that little boy ... we're getting to the stage where we're going to have to think about excluding him soon."

We looked at the *aged debt report* only to see that this family, along with many others had debts of several thousand pounds, much of which was greater than 90 days overdue. In fact, the family had paid almost nothing for over six months.

The good news from this tale, is they implemented all of the systems which I've detailed in the rest of this chapter, including managed fee collection systems and exclusion policies. When I visited them about two years ago (about eight years after the previous visit) they had no bad debt and almost no overdue accounts. They have actually become one of the most successful nurseries I know.

FEE COLLECTION SYSTEMS

Almost without exception, larger chains of nurseries only accept payment through vouchers and *Direct Debit*. They do this because they know how tough it is to get regular payments out of parents without a huge amount of difficulty.

Indeed, *Direct Debit* is the chosen method of collection for most repetitive payment systems these days from gym membership through to telecoms and utilities. Many companies in general and many childcare settings even charge a premium if you don't pay by *Direct Debit*.

And it's not difficult to understand why *Direct Debit* is such a popular choice.

Firstly it means that payments are received in a timely manner without chasing. The impact on cash received is, therefore, immense. Just consider how much time you spend chasing parents for fees. If you don't use *Direct Debit,* I suspect it's significant.

Secondly, unlike systems such as standing orders, *Direct Debits* can be varied each month which allows them to be used after fee increases and/or any other form of variation of an invoice.

But the time taken to chase late paying customers is not the real problem. The real problem is the hidden effect it has on the success of your business and the way you manage your cash.

If cash in not coming in promptly, you may have to borrow or access an overdraft to cover the cash shortfall. *Direct Debit* eliminates the majority (though not all) of the need for chasing parents for payment.

Larger nurseries who have been trading for some time will be able to get a *Direct Debit* system from their bank. For smaller nurseries, pre-schools and childminders managed *Direct Debit* systems are available from most of the software vendors on the market including *Parenta.*

There are two big advantages of using a managed *Direct Debit* system.

Firstly a managed system will automatically apply a fine to parents whose *Direct Debits* fail (like most other financial institutions) to cover the costs of a second collection and as a disincentive to allow the *Direct Debit* to fail again.

Secondly, but incredibly importantly, it separates the setting from the fee collection process. If you have a personal relationship with parents (pretty likely if you see them every day) it becomes difficult to apply fines and penalties; after all, the reason they choose your warm, caring attitude. A third party collection system allows you to blame *the system.*

Do not underestimate the advantage this would give you.

INTRODUCING NEW PAYMENT SYSTEMS

Many settings are apprehensive about introducing more rigid forms of fee collection. They fear they will lose customers.

Having been involved with hundreds of settings who have introduced a managed *Direct Debit* fee collection system over a period of more than ten years, I can assure you that this is hardly ever the case.

Most Childcare owners I speak to after they have installed a managed *Direct Debit* fee collection system are surprised about how positive parents are about paying this way (why wouldn't they be, most other bills are paid this way and people generally want less hassle).

There are ways to introduce such systems which minimise the impact and support parents' choice. When introducing *Direct Debit,* many settings increase their fees and then discount them back down for those who pay by *Direct Debit.*

This is not only a shrewd psychological game, it's cheaper for parents to pay by *Direct Debit*, but it also covers the additional administrative costs for those parents who refuse to pay in this manner.

Other successful settings have a fixed fee surcharge for all payments that are not paid via *Direct Debit* or vouchers.

Fee collection via *Direct Debit* is a massive win for both the parents and the providers. Use it if you possibly can.

ACCURATE MONTHLY BILLING

Successful settings ensure that their billing is accurate, undertaken *monthly* and that invoices are transmitted electronically to parents. Some settings, are, however, still invoicing *weekly* or *termly.*

Both of these billing frequencies cause problems for your setting.

Weekly billing adds a huge administrative burden to the setting. Not only do you have to manage your billing run 4.3 times more per month, but then you have to collect the payment more frequently which has a significant extra cost in bank charges and other fees as well as time spent chasing parents.

Billing termly has other problems. Unless your invoices are very small, most parents who are billed termly end up actually paying monthly. So, immediately your debt management becomes difficult because you won't know who to chase as some parents will pay over time. It then makes it quite difficult to catch those people who are falling behind or pay later than agreed.

My strong recommendation is therefore that you should always bill monthly in advance for standard sessions and collecting all incidentals in arrears, or as they are consumed.

MAKE SURE YOU UNDERSTAND THE COSTS OF FEE COLLECTION

I went to a small chain of nurseries the other day. We were talking about fee collection and how much various collection methods cost.

In the main, they used standing order, but also used cheques and a credit card collection facility.

Credit card collection immediately raised my concern. I presumed that meant just for incidentals. I was wrong.

It turned out they were using credit cards to collect full-time monthly fees.

I asked if they meant *Debit* cards?

Again, I was wrong.

Let's think this through with a worked example.

Again, let's use the magic £1,000 per month for a full-time place.

Credit cards vary but cost between 0.75% and 2.75% for *MasterCard* or *Visa* and as much as 3.05% for *American Express (AmEx)*. So on a £1,000 invoice, you'd be paying between £7.50 and £27.50 for *Mastercard* or *Visa*, and an incredible £30.50 for *AmEx*.

So, the annual cost of collecting fees using this method for one parent of a full-time child is between £90 and £366 per year!

This is *crazy money* for fee collection!

The argument was, at least the chain got their money promptly. A *Direct Debit* service would cost them between £10.50 and £21 per year per child, and the money would be in their bank on the same day each month.

That's a saving of between £79.50 and £345 per child, per year.

And so the moral of this story is; you can't afford to collect your fees by credit card, *unless* you pass these fees onto parents. The most effective solution is *Direct Debit*.

Use it.

Either use a managed *Direct Debit* collection service from one of the software vendors or get your own *Direct Debit* system from your bank.

PREVENTING BAD DEBT

Many settings I visit have a problem with bad debt, and so the good news (if you can call it that) is, if you have bad debt, you're not alone.

I'd go so far as to say that bad debt has reached epidemic proportions within our sector, and we all need to up our game to overcome it.

Bad debt is when a customer leaves your setting and hasn't paid you the money they should have. Invariably, it occurs when fee collection systems are not robust, deposits are insufficient, and, inevitably, because you are too nice!

But what's the real cost of bad debt? Unfortunately, it's significantly greater than most people realise?

Let's assume that your business has a 5% profit margin and that a parent has left you owing £1,000. £1,000 is a lot of money in anyone's book, but in your case, it's actually a lot more. In order to *earn* that £1,000 with a 5% margin you would have needed to invoice £20,000!

Let's go through that equation.

With a 5% margin, you earn 1/20th of everything you bill (100/5=20). So, if you multiply that £1,000 of bad debt by 20, you get back to the *earned value*.

Quite simply then, you cannot afford to not have adequate and robust debt collection systems in place and you need to implement your bad-debt systems as soon as you are aware of a problem.

The most successful chains rarely suffer from bad debt. They achieve this by:

- Making substantial deposits for fee paying parents mandatory. This protects the business if the parent leaves without paying.
- Having robust terms and conditions that make it absolutely clear to parents what the processes are

for payment, what fees are charged for late payment and what will happen if the child leaves the setting without the requisite notice period.

- Having clear and explicit Child exclusion policies.
- Having clear and explicit processes for chasing bad debt.

DEPOSITS

Are you taking a deposit from all of your fee-paying parents? If not, it's vitally important that you do.

Deposits are a necessity throughout life. You pay them when you rent a car or take a tenancy on a house, or when you hire equipment. Even at a hotel, they take a swipe of your credit card to cover the extras - as a deposit.

Use the same logic in your childcare setting. Parents should pay a deposit to protect you from them leaving owing you money and this should be at least equivalent to one month's fees.

TERMS AND CONDITIONS

I am frequently baffled at how poor most provider's terms and conditions are. Successful settings have terms and conditions that work for them.

They set out how much notice the parent must give to remove their child or to decrease their number of sessions, they define clearly how much deposit is required and when it will be returned. They clearly state the costs associated with late collection, and the costs relating to paying if the parent doesn't use the standard methods.

CHILD EXCLUSION POLICIES

The couple who ran a small chain of nurseries didn't exclude the children whose parents hadn't paid for many months. This issue nearly cost them the business.

Successful settings recognise that they must have child exclusion policies if the parent fails to pay.

POLICIES

Successful settings have clear bad debt policies they action as soon as a bad-debt becomes apparent.

IDENTIFYING DEBT

One of the most important aspects for any business owner, especially those in Childcare, is to keep a watchful eye on how much debt you have at any point. In the national survey *Parenta* undertook in September 2014, *'What Key Performance Indicators Do You Measure?',* only 3% of respondents monitored and tracked their outstanding fees.

The best way to track and measure fees is to pull an *aged debt* report from your management software.

The *aged debt* report details the amounts that each parent owes you, and shows it in categories of 0-30 days, 31-60 days and 61-90 days and 90+ days.

This report should be pulled at least weekly, and you should take action for anyone over 30 days.

Businesses go bust invariably through insufficient cash and cash management is a key to avoiding this scenario.

Once you have identified any debts over 30 days old, it's important you have a strategy to deal with them, and that you implement it straight away.

DEALING WITH BAD DEBT

Once you have a bad debt, it is essential that you deal with it immediately; so having predetermined processes are a must. Your bad debt process should include:

- A letter to the parents giving them 14 days notice to clear the debt before you pass the matter to your legal team.
- A letter at day seven reminding the parent that they have just seven days left to clear the debt.
- On day zero, you should send a *Letter before action*. A letter before action is a legal letter from a firm of solicitors advising that action is about to be taken. There are many services of this nature on the internet, and it should only cost you a couple of pounds.

Once a letter-before-action has been dispatched, the legal firm usually then has a series of processes that allow you, relatively painlessly, to pursue the matter through the courts.

At *Parenta*, we use a company called *Thomas Higgins and Co* which has a fully automated process.

REVENUE LEAKAGE AND WASTAGE

My youngest daughter attends the after-school club of a small local chain. She goes there regularly, two or three times a week. She's picked up from school at 3:30pm and stays there for a couple of hours before being collected before 6pm. She loves it there as she's able to spend even more time with her best friend.

Occasionally, though, we need her to attend for an extra afternoon beyond the normal routine. This happens maybe six or eight times a year.

Now, before I go on with the story, I should say that I know the MD well and kept a record of all the extra times my daughter attended. I say this because, for nearly six months, I never paid for the extra sessions.

And it wasn't because I was being difficult – it was because I was never asked to pay! The standard monthly invoice did not include anything for these ad-hoc sessions: simply, the company was failing to bill. And the funny thing was, every time I saw the MD, I asked him if he had revenue leakage within the business.

He assured me he didn't.

After nearly six months, I was too embarrassed to allow it to continue so I 'fessed up and paid up. But it's a sorry tale that I suspect is happening often. To this end, go and find out what extra sessions or ad-hoc sessions occurred in your nursery or after-school-club within the last month and double check that you actually raised an invoice and have been paid. Remember, the MD in this example was adamant that he did not have a problem!

The story goes on, though. A year or so after I came clean, the chain was acquired by one of the largest chains in the country. Everything remained the same from our perspective: same premises, same staff etc. The only thing that changed significantly was the old mini-bus that collected my daughter from school was replaced with a nice shiny new one.

Oh, and one more thing, the new company stopped parents booking ad-hoc extra sessions.

Now, they have excess capacity.

And they clearly have market demand: My family occasionally needs ad-hoc, unplanned cover so I'm pretty sure there are others.

But now they will only take bookings two weeks in advance! They are, therefore, 'happy' to turn away all of the ad-hoc, unplanned care that parents want!

This issue is all about poor policy.

Given that there are no additional costs in running the

service (staff and premises are already sunk costs) and they have the capacity, the revenue from these ad-hoc bookings would fall straight to the bottom line.

So, due to some policy that prevents parents from booking what they need, when they need it, they simply turn the business away.

That's revenue wastage. Actually, it's worse than that. It's profit wastage!

CONCLUSION

For every business, cash is king. As soon as you start to run out of cash, life becomes hard, and the viability of the business is jeopardised. It's no different for your childcare business. Having cash to pay bills on time is critical.

Successful childcare providers ensure they have sufficient cash by making collecting fees an automated process. They use an automated fee collection service, such as *Direct Debit* or a managed *Direct Debit* service to remove not only the hassle of collecting fees but equally the delays involved with chasing parents for cheques etc.

Successful providers, collect their normal fees monthly in advance and collect the incidentals monthly in arrears. They avoid fee collection problems, by combining automated collection facilities and holding a sensible deposit with robust terms and conditions.

Significantly, they are paranoid about revenue leakage and regularly check to ensure that everything is billed correctly.

Lastly, but perhaps most importantly of all, the most successful settings don't have bad debt. They don't have bad debt because they simply don't allow it to happen. They have taken many of the actions listed and actively exclude children as soon as any debt is equal to the deposit held.

KEY POINTS

1. Ensure you have robust terms and conditions which clearly set out how and when you will deal with late payments. Too many nurseries I visit seem to treat terms and conditions as an afterthought; they are rarely well written, seldom highlight key terms and are often not fully explained to parents. In contrast, the most successful nurseries:

- Ensure that their terms and conditions are well written and detail exactly how and when payments should be made, when payments become late, what the consequences are of late payments and, most importantly, that they will exclude the child from the setting if a payment is more than x days late.

- Ensure that these key terms are highlighted within the document (and I mean that they are highlighted in bright yellow so that there is no opportunity for the parent to miss them).

- Ensure that they go through these terms and conditions, and highlight the payment clauses during the induction session. They also ensure that the parent *signs* the terms and conditions *and initials* the payment terms during the induction. This way, there can be no opportunity for the parent to say that they didn't know when payments are due or the consequences of not paying.

2. Always collect regular fees in advance. Some settings are still collecting fees in arrears. This is the wrong way to approach this subject, as not only does this affect your cash flow, but equally at the end of the month you will have no security for the parent to pay. The most successful settings:

- Only ever collect regular fees in advance. There are no exceptions.

- Allow any extras to be collected in arrears, or as consumed.

3. For fee-paying parents, hold a sensible deposit, and *only* return it once the child has left the setting and all fees have been paid. Again, too many settings I see hold a very small deposit and often allow struggling parents to use the deposit in lieu of fees due. The most successful nurseries:

- Maintain a full deposit for the duration of the child's education
- Only return the deposit once the child has left the setting and all payments are up-to-date
- Never allow parents to use the deposit to offset fees (which so often happens for the last payment)
- Ensure the deposit is always *equal to or greater than* one month's fees (i.e. if the number of regular sessions increases, so too should the deposit)

4. Use an automated fee collection system. Collecting fees via cash and cheque and individual bank transfers is antiquated, extremely difficult to control, difficult to keep track off, and in many cases, difficult for parents to manage. In this day and age, most people prefer to have regular bills paid via automated payment systems such as direct debit or automated debit card payments. Automated systems *(like Parenta's fee collection service)* not only collect fees via direct debit every month but automatically address any non-collections by charging the parent a fee for a late payment and re-submitting the *Direct Debit* a few days later. The most successful nurseries:

- Only collect payments via automated payment systems and vouchers. They do not accept payments any other way. They do this because they understand the *real* cost of late payments.

- Never allow parents to bypass their regular payment systems.
- Always charge parents for late payments (by using automated collection systems).
- Never *ever* collect regular fees via a credit card, unless you are adding the costs of credit card processing on top of the invoice value.

5. Monitor all late payments via the Aged Balance Report from their nursery management system, and take immediate, pre-determined action once a payment becomes late. Many settings are not using aged balance reports to measure and monitor their late payments and then do not have systems in place to deal with those late payments. The most successful settings:

- Review their aged balance report weekly and take action against anyone whose payment is over two weeks old.
- Have pre-determined policies for late payment which they implement immediately a payment is over two weeks old.
- Use their pre-determined processes to write to parents at regular intervals about late payments and are willing to exclude children whose parent's payments are late.
- Never *ever* let a late payment exceed the holding deposit.
- Engage a debt collection service as soon as a debt becomes a bad debt (i.e. when the child has been removed from the setting and a debt is overdue by more than one month).

6. Invoice monthly. Whilst the majority of settings now invoice monthly, there are many who still offer some parents weekly billing terms and a few who still invoice termly.

Weekly billing adds an enormous additional strain to your workload and makes keeping on top of payments more difficult. In contrast, termly billing makes management information more difficult to understand and distorts your profit and loss account unnecessarily. It also puts a huge strain on parents to pay in a lump sum and consequently most parents end up paying monthly; in turn, this makes managing your debt, even more difficult. Successful settings:

- Invoice monthly in advance for regular sessions, and in arrears for any extras.

7. Be paranoid about revenue leakage wastage. Are you absolutely sure you are billing for everything, including all ad-hoc sessions and all extras? Successful settings:

- Regularly check that they don't have any revenue leakage.
- Review their businesses to ensure that opportunities for extra revenue and extra profit are not squandered, by policies that make no sense.

Al's Rant

Bad debt is a major problem throughout the sector.

One reason is we choose to hide it by giving it a 'nice' name. It's not bad debt, it's theft. Pure and simple theft. But it's theft we as a sector can control. Implementing the processes I have outlined that the most successful settings use, will make a huge difference to the profitability of the whole sector.

CHAPTER SEVEN: FINANCE

"When it comes to finances, nothing is more dangerous than flying blind." Michael Hyatt

The *Parenta National Childcare Survey* produced some interesting findings about *Finance*. Half of the respondents felt they had their finance systems under control, and half did not. Either way, my experience of working with many nurseries has identified that successful nurseries think about their costs in different ways; and focus on revenue maximisation above all else.

Key Finding

Successful settings and more forward thinking businesses determine in advance how much money they want to make in a given period. They then structure their businesses to maximise revenue opportunities through differential pricing, or through optimising sessions. They understand the *real* costs of running their business, and how to use them to their advantage.

- Is you childcare business making the level of profit you want, need or expect?
- Are you waiting to see how much profit you make at the end of the year, or are you driving the business to achieve the results you want?

- Do you have instant information about how your business is performing?
- How do you maximise the revenue opportunities within your business?

IT'S TIME TO START THINKING ABOUT PROFIT FIRST!

As we know, 49% of nurseries expect to make a loss or only break even during the year.

Part of the problem within the sector is how profit is perceived.

Ingrained with every business manager is the age-old adage:

$$Sales - Expenses = Profit$$

Makes sense? It's what we all work to and we all understand. It's what we all use to calculate the results of our businesses.

And yet, what if it were wrong? What if this equation were completely incorrect, and we'd all been looking at our businesses the wrong way round.

Well, the most successful businesses determine in advance the profit that they want to make in a year, and then work on increasing revenue, or decreasing expenses to achieve this result.

And so for *these* businesses, the equation is changed. It now reads:

$$Sales - Profit = Expenses$$

Now, many will say this is the same equation and logically it is. But from a *behavioural* perspective, *everything* has changed.

With the new equation, if you fix profit at a certain level, you need to either increase your sales, or decrease your costs: they are the only two options you have, and this inevitably changes how you think about both. Profit is no longer whatever is left over.

It is however often very difficult to reduce your costs. The largest costs for your setting will be staff, and reducing staff costs, whilst maintaining ratios is hard. The second largest cost is probably rent (or mortgage) and rates. Again, it's unlikely that these can be easily reduced. And in any case, as you keep trying to reduce costs, there comes a point in cost reduction where the viability of the business is jeopardised.

Nonetheless, most businesses are surprised at how much they can take out of the business if they really try.

However, it's easier to increase revenues than to cut costs, which is why I have emphasised running at full capacity within the previous chapters.

PRODUCT EXTENSION

What should you do to increase profits if you are at, or close to, full capacity? In this case, you can open another setting, although there are a myriad of issues associated with that. There are however other solutions.

When faced with full capacity, the most successful nurseries embark on other strategies.

Firstly, they increase their prices. We'll talk about price in *Chapter 8*, where I'll explain the real issues around price increases.

Secondly, they increase the spend per family by adding ancillary products and services to their offering. The obvious service extension is after-school clubs, but successful settings often increase their services more comprehensively by offering significantly later opening hours if demand suggests it, by offering extra services such as parties at weekends or using the space for clubs in the evenings.

Others extend their services by offering café style facilities, or by tying in with other local businesses and taking a margin for, say, offering pre-cooked meals for the evening or as a drop-off point for dry cleaning.

The most successful nurseries also team up with local children's entertainers, language tutors and music tutors offering them the use of the premises either during the day or at weekends allowing parents to book these for their children whilst taking a percentage for themselves. Finally, successful nurseries also offer classes for parents on their premises such as paediatric first aid or learning through play, again adding additional revenue.

It's interesting to note that 4% of the respondents to the *NDNA's 2016 Annual Nursery Survey* are open on a Saturday. Those settings saw a Saturday as having similar occupancy rates to normal weekdays.

This is another ideal way of extending revenue opportunities with only a small increase in costs, though it does often make staff deployment much more challenging.

WHY YEAR-TO-DATE (YTD) AND TRADITIONAL BUDGETING IS FLAWED

Beyond increasing revenues, it important to look at budgeting so that you are not flying blind.

The majority of business look at their profit and loss account each month and are either incredibly pleased or incredibly frustrated. But they think of the *P&L* in isolation – as a single point in time, not as a trend of what's happening.

Often on the profit and loss sheet from the major accountancy vendors, you have the ability to see your financial results for the current month and *Year-to-Date (YTD)*. And whilst looking at results on a *YTD* basis is the most common method, it is also the least effective.

YTD only measures the businesses performance over a full year, once. So only at month 12 do you see the full *YTD* picture. For the remaining 11 months, it is measuring an incomplete year and thereby exposing the user to seasonal variation. It's also an ineffective tool for decision making because it displays past information and sheds no light on current or future business conditions.

Likewise, traditional budgeting is flawed. Traditional budgeting works by companies producing a budget during an annual budgeting process. After each month concludes they record their results and track their progress towards or against the original forecast. They then spend precious time and energy trying to explain the variances to a budget when, inevitability, circumstances have changed *after* the budget was created. So while this traditional process is better than not budgeting at all, it has minimal real value.

FORECASTING AHEAD

Forecasting is never 100% accurate. Indeed, the only thing we do know for certainty about any forecast is it must be wrong in some way because conditions are changing all the time. New information and revised market conditions make original estimates less and less accurate with each passing month. *YTD* and traditional budgeting don't take this into account.

But the most successful businesses do use forecasting and do so in a way which is meaningful, and as accurate as possible. They track their results using systems that highlight trends and remove seasonal fluctuations. It's called the *Trailing Twelve Month (TTM)* method.

TTM is a moving measurement that includes the most recent twelve months of results instead of looking at an individual month or *YTD*. This is incredibly powerful, and most importantly, incredibly valuable to any company subject to significant seasonal variations as we are in Childcare.

And it's incredibly easy to calculate. Just add together the previous 12 months results and plot them on a chart. Next month, add the previous 12-month results, and so on. (Further examples of how to set-up *TTM* are included within *Chapter 11*).

The most successful businesses do much more, however.

The most successful businesses use the *24 Month Rolling (24MR)* system.

24MR incorporates the *Trailing Twelve-month (TTM)* method and adds in a further 12 months of predictions to give an even clearer view of performance, looking at the past, present and future within a single view. At the end of every month, the new prediction for the new month 12 is added to the system, whilst the last month minus 12 falls off the end. So effectively, you have a permanent view of 12 months in the past and 12 months into the future.

This enables setting owners to ask the following every month, *'What information has come to light in the last 30 days that changes our view of the future?'* Amending the view of the future then just requires you to update your forecast accordingly.

YOUR OWN TIME MACHINE

The *24MR* system is an amazingly powerful mechanism that allows you to determine your own future. If you don't like what you are seeing as the results for 12 months time, you know that you can start to make amendments *now* to see how you can adjust the future. It's your own time machine. It allows you to jump forward to 12 months in the future to see what lies ahead, and then to zip back to today to make any necessary amendments that you need to.

Successful settings and businesses use this system to manipulate their results so they can achieve the profit level they desire. They model the impact on their profit levels

12 months in advance by adjusting the key levers within their business today.

THE SEVEN KEY FINANCIAL LEVERS

There are seven financial levers that any business can adjust which will impact on the financial results of the company. Successful businesses exploit these levers to manipulate their results and model the outcomes within their *24MR* forecasting systems.

1. REVENUE COLLECTION

I've dealt with the critical issues of collecting fees within *Chapter 6*. Within this section though it's worth highlighting that bringing in money sooner has an impact on the operational cash within the business. We've yet to use the term *operational cash,* but this is the cash you have available to manage the business. Operational cash is also sometimes known as cash flow.

2. INVENTORY MANAGEMENT

Inventory is any products you hold in stock for future use. Many settings purchase food and consumables in bulk as it's cheaper. Whilst this is true, more successful setting recognise that purchasing products this way has a negative impact on operational cash, as cash is *stored* in these products rather than being used for something else. Keeping inventory to a minimum frees up operational cash allowing you to use it elsewhere.

3. ACCOUNTS PAYABLE (CREDITORS)

Accounts payable is the American term for *Creditors*. Whilst those who have an accountancy background will prefer the term *creditors*, my experience suggests that many setting owners get confused between creditors and their counterpart, debtors, and so I prefer to use the term accounts payable as *'it does what it says on the tin'*. It is those accounts or bills that you need to pay.

More successful nurseries and businesses use accounts payable wisely. If they are cash rich, then they may negotiate better rates with suppliers to pay bills early. In contrast, if they are cash poor then they may choose to stretch payment terms to free up more cash.

4. PRICE STRATEGY

We're covering pricing strategy in *Chapter 8*. Never underestimate though the impact that a small increase in price can have on your profitability.

5. VOLUME STRATEGY

This is about increasing the occupancy of your setting to maximise its capacity.

6. DIRECT COST CONTROL

Direct costs are those costs which vary depending on the number of children in the setting. As the number of children increases so does direct costs. Examples of what may be direct costs are food, nappies, aprons, gloves etc.

7. INDIRECT COST CONTROL

Indirect costs are those that are constant, irrespective of the volume of children. So this would include all the costs of permanent staff, premises costs including rates and utilities and any other fixed costs.

USING SUNK COSTS AS A SOURCE OF COMPETITIVE ADVANTAGE

As we have just discussed, indirect costs are those expenses which you incur irrespective of the amount of children you have in your setting. These are also called sunk costs, as they have to be paid irrespective of how well the business is performing.

Many settings look at these costs as a negative. *'If only I didn't have to pay X,Y or Z we would be making money'* is a regular cry.

More successful settings recognise, that sunk costs *can be* an opportunity for competitive advantage, and use these costs accordingly.

In *Chapter 4*, I relayed the story that settings don't often ask for the business, and how you can use sunk costs to your advantage by offering a month's free childcare without it *really* costing you anything.

If you take the logic from that example, you can use sunk costs to your advantage, though this does require a mind-set change.

Many providers are stuck in the mind-set of looking at everything on a cost per hour basis. And this is not surprising given that they are paid this way from Local Authorities and we all contract staff based on the number of hours they work.

Successful businesses don't look at costs in this way, though. They step back and look at the total costs of running the business. By accepting that the total costs are fixed or sunk (subject to the cost reduction we talked about earlier) they know that they can use this to their advantage. Go back to the story in *Chapter 4* to better understand how.

MANAGEMENT ACCOUNTS (FINANCIAL STATEMENTS)

If your intention is to run your business profitably you will need to understand *Management Accounts* (or *Financial Statements*). Management accounts include:

- The *Balance Sheet* (which measures the *value* of your business at a set point in time).
- The *Income Statement* (or *Profit and Loss Statement* which measures the *vitality* of your business over time).
- *Operational Cash* (or *Cash Flow Statement*, which measures the *viability* of your business).

Many small business owners don't create a set of management accounts and use them to make important business decisions, because they don't know how to read them.

THE BALANCE SHEET

The *Balance Sheet* - generated monthly - lists your *assets* and *liabilities* from the time you started your business, along with other useful numbers. Importantly, it tells you the *value* of your business *As At* a specific point in time like the first or last trading day of the month.

A typical Balance Sheet will include:

- *Total Funding - Cash-At-Bank;* and *Cash/Debt/Loans.*
- *Total Capital Employed - Fixed Capital* and *Working Capital (tax liabilities, creditors, debtors, and inventory).*

As such it provides a necessary overview of the financial strength of your business.

INCOME STATEMENT (PROFIT AND LOSS STATEMENT)

Your *Income Statement* (or *Profit and Loss Statement* or simply *the P&L)* shows the *revenues* you have generated from a given period; deducts the *costs of doing business* (if applicable) to determine your *gross profit;* then deducts your *overheads*, tax and *costs of finance*; which results in your *net profit for the period*.

The *P&L* importantly measures the *vitality* of your business.

If the resulting number is positive, you've made a *profit*, and if it's negative, you've made a *loss*.

Simple isn't it? Well, actually, no it isn't. This is because within the costs element you will need to allow for factors like depreciation and interest.

Let's look at the revenues element first.

A typical Profit and Loss account looks like the following.

Profit and Loss Account for ABC Nursery January 20xx		
Revenues (Total Sales)	£125,000	
Less Direct Expenses (Costs of Good Sold)		(£5,000)
Gross Profit	£120,000	
Staffing Costs include National Insurance Contribution (NIC)		(£100,000)
Rent		(£4,000)
Rates		(£1,000)
Utilities		(£1,000)
Depreciation		(£500)
Interest		(£400)
Systems & Insurance		(£250)
Net Profit	£12,500	

Your *revenues* (or *sales*) are the *total amount of money* you have billed in the given period. Usually, this would be one month, and, as discussed previously, I would recommend that this is how you should bill your parents.

So that's the sum of all of your invoices to parents, including the monies you will receive from your Local Authority for *Free Entitlement*.

If you bill termly, however, then you'll need to be careful, as you'll need to determine how much of that billed revenue relates to the given month. (As already discussed, billing termly makes your life significantly more complicated in almost every respect, including with your customers. My advice would be to avoid it if possible.)

In a traditional business, you would then deduct any costs from the billed revenue, which were truly variable as a function of the number of sales made. This would provide you with your *gross profit*.

In a childcare business, however, the only truly variable cost is likely to be food and disposables and I would suggest that this is not worth considering in this context.

You then need to deduct all of the invoices you have received for the given period, as well as all of your employment costs, including employers *National Insurance Contribution (NIC)*, and any interest paid on loans and any depreciation.

The final figure then is the net profit or loss that your business has made for the period.

Many small nursery owners I meet still find confusion around the terms net profit and gross profit, so it's worth explaining.

Net profit (or loss) is the amount left over after the subtraction of all costs from revenue. It's also frequently referred to as the *bottom line*.

Gross profit, however, is revenue *less* any truly variable costs which occur as a function of sales. Unless you use bank staff often, gross profit isn't a massively useful number for a childcare business, as it's rare to have many costs which are truly variable as sales increase or decrease. As already mentioned, the only truly variable costs are food and disposables.

OPERATIONAL CASH

Too many Childcare owners complain that they had a good month of revenues but they have no cash! And yes, you may have had a good month and even registered a good net profit but *it is not yet cash.*

Here's why.

You have to allow for any activity in the *Balance Sheet* especially *Working Capital* (e.g., taxes, accounts receivables, accounts payables, inventory purchases) as well as any major *Fixed Capital* purchases such as new a computer, to determine your *Operating Cash Flow* and subsequent *Net Cash Flow* position

Once you have allowed for those *Balance Sheet* transactions it finally becomes your actual cash-at-bank.

Many of the Childcare providers I meet easily confuse the *Profit and Loss Statement (P&L)* with *Operational Cash* or *Cash Flow* as it's often called.

In fact, some time ago I worked with two very successful nursery owners who had sold their chain of nurseries for a vast amount of money, and still struggled to understand the difference between a *Profit and Loss Statement* and *Cash Flow,* so this confusion is common.

Be sure to have absolute clarity between the two.

The *Cash Flow Statement* (often referred to as just *Cash Flow)* shows the total amount of money received by the business in a given period (usually a month) less the amount of money paid out in the same period.

So the money received would be the total amount that you have received in your bank account and not the amount that you have billed. Due to late payments, or bad-debt, or depreciation, there is usually a discrepancy between the two.

Also, as discussed in the previous section, improving your accounts receivable makes a big difference to your cash flow.

The cost paid out is the total amount of money you have paid out for the business. This would include all the bills you paid in the period, plus your staff including *Pay As You Earn (PAYE)* and *National Insurance Contributions (NIC)*, plus any loans you have plus any interest you have paid.

So cash flow is all the money you have received, less all the money you have paid out.

Profit (or loss) is determined by looking at what you billed in the month (not what you received) less all of the costs you have been invoiced for (not what you paid out) including staffing costs.

It's important to remember that profit doesn't equal available (or operational) cash. And profit doesn't equal cash flow in a business.

To find out if you made a profit or had a loss for the year, you look at the bottom line in your *P&L* (profit and loss) report.

But the bottom line does not tell your cash flow from your profit-making activities.

Don't assume that making profit increases cash by the same amount, either. A business's cash flow can be considerably higher than bottom-line profit, or considerably lower. Cash flow can be negative when you earn a profit, and cash flow can be positive when you have a loss. There's no immediate correlation between profit and cash flow.

MANAGING CASH

I've written above about the critical relevance of revenue collection and accounts payable when running your setting. The question then arises as, how you track and trend these metrics, and more importantly how do you benefit from its impact.

Here's a neat little trick that will allow you to trend these metrics easily and can have a lifesaving effect for any providers with cash flow issues.

Firstly, work your *weekly cash-turnover.* This is very simple.

Take you *total annual turnover (total Revenue)* and divide it by 12 (months). Then divide that amount by four weeks in the months. (Four is a good enough approximation).

For example, with a setting turning over £600,000 per year, this would be

- £600,000/12 = £50,000 per month.
- Then divide by 4.
- £50,000/4 = £12,500 per week.

So, the weekly cash turnover is £12,500 per week.

Now, let's assume that this setting is owed £62,500 (Debtors)

And owes £40,000 (creditors, or Accounts Payable)

If we divide both of these numbers by the weekly cash amount of £12,500, we then have a metric to follow and trend.

- Debtors - £62,500/£12,500 = 5
- Creditors - £40,000/£12,500 = 3.2

Now, for every whole number that Debtors goes down or Creditors goes up your available operating cash increases by £12,500!!

Move both metrics by one unit, and you increase operating cash by £25,000.

Now, let's say you are struggling for cash? If you implement this system, you suddenly have a lot more cash available.

Not struggling for cash, but have an overdraft? Just think how much you'd save on interest, and how much easier would it be if you didn't have to make those repayments?

To move the needle on debtors quickly and easily, implement the fee collection systems I talked about in *Chapter 6.* It will save you money!

WHY YOU NEED ROBUST
FINANCIAL MANAGEMENT INFORMATION

Whatever business you run, you need to have a clear picture of where you are at all times. Childcare is no different, you need to see, on a monthly basis how your business is performing.

In doing so, you can determine where you need to divert your attention to ensure that you start to make a respectable profit and gain a reward for all your hard work.

Once you have your financial information, you need to do something with it.

In *Chapter 11* we will talk about having a dashboard of information.

Your financial dashboard should cover the following:

- **Revenue:** You should trend your revenue every month so that you can understand how you are performing against previous periods, and understand the impact of seasonality on your numbers.

- **Net profit:** A trend of these numbers will help you understand how much profit your business is generating, or how much loss, and whether this figure is increasing or decreasing.

- **Cash flow:** This is the most important metric of all. You need to measure how much money is coming into and out of your business each month.

CUSTOMER RETENTION

Retaining customers is a key element for any business and is no less for those dealing with parents and children.

To put this in context, according to Jameson and Watson's research, businesses which have implement successful customer retention strategies report that a 2% improvement in retention has the same profit impact as a 10% reduction in overheads.

Keeping customers is just good business sense especially when you consider:

- The real cost of attracting new customers is always greater than keeping your existing customers.
- Loyal Customers always spend more on additional products and services.
- Loyal customers are willing to accept premium pricing.
- The time taken dealing with disgruntled parents is reduced.
- Loyal customers promote your services.

As part of your dashboard, you should measure customer retention rates. It is a critical metric that lets you know how well your business is being perceived by customers. If you are leaking customers, then seeing this metric will highlight the fact that you need to do something about it!

Customer retention is calculated as follows:

- Look at the number of children who were enrolled a year ago and deduct any children who graduated, and any new children added in the last year. The result is your customer retention rate.

Measure this every month (by going back 12 months as discussed in *Chapter 11,* and trend the results).

REDUCING UNNECESSARY COST

It is highly likely that you will look at your setting and say there are not a lot of unnecessary costs.

However, the one cost that you can remove is the cost of having to recruit new staff. This is always an expensive exercise as well as a time-consuming one.

But there are further implications as you well know, such as the broken bond between career and the young child. Indeed, one of the highest reasons for parents moving to another setting is when the child's carer moves.

The cost of staff leaving is,] therefore, significant.

It's important to create the healthy environment discussed in *Chapter 8* to minimise the impacts of staff leaving.

THE PROBLEMS WITH FLEXIBILITY AND HOURLY BILLING

Typically, new childcare owners offer as much flexibility as possible in how parents can book in their children. It's easy to see the rationale: being flexible, allowing complex booking patterns and facilitating parent's ability to simply pay for the specific hours their child attends seems like a fair and customer centric approach. You may also want to offer holiday discounts or overly generous sibling discounts. However, a strong word of caution.

Let's use the example of the larger chains of nurseries. With most chains and many successful nurseries, parents can book mornings, afternoons, or full days. Not a lot of flexibility? No, let's consider why?

The costs of running your business are relatively fixed. The costs of your main staff, rent, rates, utilities, insurances, and systems remain constant. As occupancy increases you might need more staff, but the base costs are fixed. It, therefore, costs about the same amount to run your business each day, irrespective of the number of children attending.

If you charge by the session (Morning, Afternoon, Full day) your revenues will cover the time for the full session. If you charge hourly, however, *and* the child is only in for part of the session, then you need to be *very* careful that you are still covering your costs.

Let's work through an example to make sure this is clear.

So, let's assume you charge £100 for a full day and both your morning sessions and afternoon sessions are £60 each (i.e. there's a discount for a full day).

Assume you are open from 8am til 6pm five days per week. That's a ten hour day, so £6 per hour for a morning or afternoon session, and £5 per hour for a full day. Makes sense?

Assume that the £100 per child per day rate, based on your current occupancy allows you to cover all costs, including paying yourself, and make a (very small) margin.

You need to cover £50 per child for the morning and £50 per child for the afternoon, and so when you charge £60 you are adding a small premium and making a little bit more money.

However, if you were to take a child for two hours in an afternoon and charge the higher rate of £6 per hour, then you are immediately not covering £50 per session.

Your costs are fixed, so in this instance, you are actually losing £38 for that session. (£50 session cost, less 2 x £6.)

Now, there's a small chain of nurseries we work with in Ireland that understands this concept well. They will only allow children for part-sessions when they have a matching child who can fill the remaining part of the session. They call this pairing, and it works well for them.

Unless you can pair children together, charging hourly can significantly damage your earning potential, and therefore your profitability.

And so the moral of this story is: follow the lead of the most successful nurseries by charging sessionally, irrespective of when the child attends. Simply put, charging for small blocks of hours makes it significantly harder to cover your total costs, and, impacts on your ability to become more profitable.

One last point on this issue.

Some of the most successful settings I know are considering offering only full-days for older children. They do this to relieve the pressure on staff of having multiple changeovers during the lunch window.

My point, flexibility in booking arrangements is clearly advantageous to parents, but often adds more pressure to settings, and can jeopardise profitability.

LATE FEES

If you aren't charging for late pick-ups, you really should be.

A few years ago, an article was published in *The Telegraph* (UK) suggesting nurseries are now adopting a *RyanAir* approach - providing the very basic minimum services and then charging parents for extra services like lunch and nappies.

The article suggested that childcare settings are being unethical for charging those extras which are not already covered by the core costs which parents or Local Authorities pay.

In particular, the article seems to say that nurseries are putting the squeeze on working parents by charging fees for late pickup.

Let me ask you this: are teachers expected to look after children for free after the school day has ended? No, parents must pay for an after school club! So why should parents expect to get childcare for free from a nursery?

As you well know, caring for children is a demanding, exhausting profession, so child carers should absolutely charge for late fees especially as providers must cover the additional costs associated with having to pay their staff overtime to stay later.

Parents' lateness also creates an additional inconvenience for these staff members, who may have to cancel other commitments after work in order to stay later than planned.

The only thing that does surprise me about this topic is that only one in three Childcare settings actually do choose to charge late fees!

Clearly this journalist doesn't know that just 49% of all nurseries in the UK are expected to make a profit this year?

For a long time settings have struggled with the gap between what the local authority pays them and what it actually costs to provide care. Therefore, providers cannot be blamed for trying to recoup this cost by charging parents for additional services such as late fees.

The sensationalist report by the *Citizen's Advice Bureau* referenced in the article claims that parents are having difficulties returning to work due to the inflexibility of childcare providers.

The report's findings state that nearly 60% of providers required a month or more notice to change or end arrangements. Considering that nurseries must plan ahead and make sure they always arrange adequate staffing levels for any changes in occupancy, they are actually being responsible by not allowing parents to change their childcare plans without giving them adequate notice.

I'm disappointed this journalist failed to appreciate that the childcare industry is vocational: childcare business owners go into the profession because they are passionate about providing quality childcare, not (as this journalist and the *CAB* report seem to suggest) because they are money grabbing and want to make life difficult for working parents. They must though, be profitable if they are to survive and prosper.

Every setting should be charging late fees for late collection for two reasons. Firstly, to cover additional costs, and secondly to parents to discourage this behaviour.

Late fees are not just applicable to collections at the end of the day, though. Many settings fail to implement late collection policies for those parents who collect their children late after a morning session, or any other type of session that doesn't end at closing time.

Successful settings recognise that late fees should be applicable whenever a parent fails to collect their child at the agreed time. And successful settings not only charge late payment fees every time a parent is late, irrespective of the actual time of day, they also ensure this is clearly covered within the terms and conditions.

BUY VERSES DIY

The final topic in this finance section is the BUY versus DIY approach. Owners of most small businesses, childcare or otherwise, often think they can save money by implementing solutions to common problems either themselves or by existing friends or family.

Building a website is a common example. We frequently hear from providers who have had a website built by their son, or by a parent. And usually, it was done five years or so ago.

When I ask questions, I quickly learn that their website hasn't been updated in years, it's not mobile compatible and not generating enquiries. Rarely do DIY solutions to business problems actually yield the results that are expected.

You have spent years crafting your own profession and building systems and services to make your setting effective.

The providers of systems will have done the same for whatever they are providing and will have thought through the issues and problems to deliver an effective solution.

To increase the viability and profitability of your business you need to systematise (see *Chapter 11).*

I strongly suggest thinking carefully before trying to save money on DIY solutions. My experience suggests they usually cost more in the long-run.

CONCLUSION

Our thinking is often constrained by what we know to be the established norms and what we have been taught. Conventional wisdom tells us how to calculate profit, and yet when we change the equation around our thinking is forced to change. Suddenly profit is no longer *just* what's left over, but part of a conscious, pre-determined plan.

In making profit a pre-determined fixed amount, we have no option but to change our thinking about revenues and expenses, and then to take the necessary actions.

Successful settings and successful businesses in general, use sophisticated planning systems to enable them to predict the future. These systems allow managers to use the financial levers within their control to manipulate financial results as they strive to achieve the profit they are seeking.

Particularly important is the management of accounts receivable to ensure that cash is available to fund growth, and that maximum occupancy is obtained.

Successful settings recognise the inherent dangers in offering too much flexibility to parents as they understand the real cost of not having sessions fully paid for, irrespective of whether the child is in attendance. They also recognise that parents have contracted with them for a period of time. As a consequence, if parents break that contract by being late, they actively charge late fees to dissuade parents from doing it repeatedly and to cover their additional costs.

Finally, successful settings understand that it is often advantageous to buy services in rather than try to do the work themselves. They understand that investing in a tried and tested solution is far cheaper than trying to learn how to create a solution themselves since the revenue generated by the solution impacts the business so much quicker.

KEY POINTS

1. Reconsider how you think about profit. Rather, than leaving profit to be whatever is left over, make a conscious decision in advance about the level of profit you want to achieve and adjust your business accordingly.

- Abandon ineffective budgeting and start using *24MR* to give you a full view of how your business is performing looking at the past 12 months and next 12 months in one comprehensive system.
- Use *TTM*, within *24MR* to ensure that you are removing the seasonality associated with our sector.
- Use the financial levers within your control to adjust your results.

2. Understand the difference between cash flow and profit and loss. Cash is the lifeblood of your business and you must understand that lack of cash will undermine your ability to develop the business, and can threaten your setting's survival. This means investing in infrastructure and your staff, is jeopardised.

3. Be careful about hourly billing and adding too much flexibility. Reducing the availability of your services to full days and morning/afternoon sessions allows to you fully cover your overheads irrespective of the hours the child attends. Successful settings recognise this and offer services that work for them. They also do not offer excessive discount structures. If they do offer flexibility they try to *pair* children to ensure that full days are always achieved. Some successful settings only offer full day care to maximise revenues and eliminate the costs associated with gaps in occupancy.

4. Always charge for late pick-ups beyond the contracted or booked hours. It is entirely appropriate that you charge parents if they are late in collecting their child. You need to cover staff wages and discourage this behaviour.

5. Be careful about making your own solutions rather than buying them from appropriate vendors.

Usually, managers buy a product for the impact it has on their business. And by impact, I mean either a cost saving or revenue generating impact. I often see settings who have tried to solve the problem themselves to save money.

In the end, its false logic to try a DIY solution as the revenues or cost savings simply don't materialise as its takes too long to learn the solution, or it's implemented poorly.

I have seen so many sub-standard websites that rather than being a positive lead generation tool, end up just being an online brochure, which doesn't impact on enquiry levels or occupancy.

Al's Rant

Recently, there have been a number of new entrants into the supply side of the sector. Adding lots of new companies and increasing competition is always a good thing. Except of course, when they aren't trading ethically, or perhaps lawfully. And at that point there's the potential for settings to get damaged by losing money, or worse, losing data. To be specific, I have seen several new entrants who state they are limited companies, but in reality, they are not. Every limited company has a credit rating based on a range of factors which determine if they are suitable to trade with. If however, they are not a limited company, you simply cannot tell if they are safe to trade with. If you are investing money or time with a vendor you haven't used before, you really need to check this out in advance. It's simply not worth the risk. To my mind, if they don't have a positive credit rating, there's a reason. If not, I'd steer well clear!

CHAPTER 8: PRICING

"Price is what you pay. Value is what you get." Warren Buffett

The *Parenta National Childcare Survey* highlighted pricing as a major concern amongst providers. Many settings are reluctant to increase fees for fear of losing or upsetting customers and they rarely have a system to implement fee increases or to determine how much a fee increase should be.

> **Key Finding**
>
> Successful settings have a clear system to determine their pricing and implement fee increases without fear of customer loss. They build their pricing structure around the value they provide to customers, and they increase their fees regularly. Finally, they understand the real impact of price on their profitability.

- Do you procrastinate to increase fees?
- Do you have a system to determine a fee increase?
- Are your fee increases undertaken every year?
- Do you use variable pricing?

PRICE IS REALLY PART OF MARKETING

Price is one of the key elements in determining how your offering is perceived.

No matter what you buy, you make an assumption about quality based on price. If something is cheap, you assume it's of a lesser quality and accept it for what it is. If it's expensive, you assume the quality is high and expect it to be superior. Additionally, higher priced products and services are often seen as aspirational.

Childcare is the same. Where your offering sits on a price scale compared to your local competitors is important. You need to consider this fact as you determine your pricing policy. If you don't know what you competitors charge, it's time you found out.

Successful providers have something in common. They almost always position themselves as either the most expensive in the area, or one of the most expensive. They do this, firstly because they recognise that parents often want the best service. Secondly, they know that sitting at this point in the pricing space allows them to maximise their profits.

Too many Childcare providers choose to position themselves as not being the best, or not being quality by being too cheap. Where you choose to position your setting, consider how it reflects on what you are trying to convey to your local marketplace, and, bearing in mind the *Revenue – Profit = Expenses* equation, ensure that your pricing allows you to achieve your profit target.

Wherever you set your prices, be sure that you have included all of your costs and base it on your current occupancy. Then, as occupancy increases so does your profitability.

SETTING YOUR PRICES

Successful settings have a structure for price setting. They don't, as so many settings and businesses in general do, just make up their price, and change it randomly, as the mood takes them.

Rather, they have a structure and policy around pricing which they stick to and ties in with the market position they have chosen.

Firstly, they understand about value.

Value is the concept of exchanging a product or service for money.

If you think the value of any product is worth the exchange for money, then it's likely you'll buy it.

In contrast, if you believe the product is not worth the exchange for money, then it's likely you won't buy it.

In the case of Childcare, there is a general public perception that it is expensive. But what are we comparing it against?

The reality is parents in your area are comparing your pricing against those of your competitors, and given that there is a minimum price point already, a minimum reasonable price is expected by parents anyway.

Many settings are worried about pricing too high. When I encounter these settings I always try to put context around price. If you know that in your local area people are used to paying £10 per hour for dog walking, then £5 per hour for providing *Early Years* education suddenly seems very reasonable.

Determine your pricing based on the position you want in your marketplace, your reputation in the marketplace, and your underlying cost base. Whilst it's important to consider the prices of your competitors, don't forget that their underlying cost base may be very different from yours.

THE REAL VALUE OF A PRICE INCREASE

Many businesses don't understand the true correlation between increased fees and the impact it has on the company's net profit. Increasing fees is often seen as one of those nasty issues that we'd rather put on the back burner and avoid dealing with.

The truth is quite the reverse.

For a typical business, an increase of 5% on the top line through a price rise, adds 44% to the businesses net profit.

OK, now stop, and re-read that line.

Increasing prices by 5% increases your operating profit by 44%. This is because *all* of your costs remain fixed, whilst your revenue increases by 5%. And of course, in this context, as you profitability increases, so does your cash.

Not achieving the profit amounts you want to? Not got enough cash? You now know the impact that a price increased can have, and you can model it using the systems we described in *Chapter 7*.

Now, I know that a significant amount of your revenue is controlled by the Local Authority, but excluding that revenue still provides an enormous opportunity for most providers to increase pricing, particularly for those in England who charge for additional services.

DETERMINING YOUR PRICING

As someone who came from outside the childcare sector, one of the things that has always confused me is the absolute insistence of many providers to look at everything based on an hourly rate.

It's obvious why this occurs. We tend to pay staff based on an hourly rate (even if they have an annual salary, it's often calculated hourly, and we pay based on contracted hours), we have 15 or 30 hours of Free Entitlement, and of course, Local Authorities pay based on those *Free Entitlement* hours.

In contrast, everything else in the business is paid monthly. Rent, bills, services etc are all paid monthly. Irrespective of the number of hours you use your building in the month, you still pay the same amount. Even staff payments, whilst derived from an hourly rate, are usually paid monthly.

These two philosophies create a paradox for childcare providers. Many providers think in terms of hours, yet pay for items based on a monthly amount.

More successful businesses think in terms of the total amount of revenue (sales) that they can generate in a month as the primary focus.

We talked in the previous chapter about ensuring that you are billing in sessions and not in hours, This takes a significant step forward as it generates revenue irrespective of the hours the child actually attends.

When looking at pricing though it's important to focus on the total revenue in the period, (say a month), against the costs for this period.

Then as revenues increase due to increased occupancy, and costs remain (practically) static, so profitability increases.

You can then use variable pricing to maximise the profit generation opportunities.

VARIABLE PRICING

I was recently reading an article about how Disney are introducing variable pricing into their theme parks.

It transpires that whilst their parks are pretty much always busy, some days they are ultra-busy and as a result, is puts a strain on maintaining their standards as well as massively increasing queue lengths, which decreases their customer's experience.

Accordingly, they are introducing a three-tiered pricing structure where they charge an increased entry fee on peak days, and a reduced entry fee on those days where visitor numbers are less than average.

So, let's spin this back to Childcare sector. Most nurseries have an attendance profile which sees them having a significantly higher occupancy level on a Wednesday than the rest of the week.

The following graph shows the average occupancy profile of a random group of 35 individual settings.

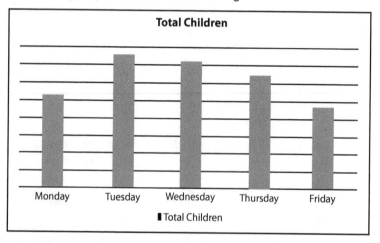

In this analysis the numbers on the *y*-axis are irrelevant. What's important is the profile, which shows clearly that Monday's and Friday's are the least popular days, with Tuesday's and Wednesdays being the most popular.

How does the attendance profile look in your setting?

Uneven attendance profiles for more successful nurseries are seen as an advantage. It allows them to offer variable pricing to make popular days more expensive and less popular days less expensive. Equally, when selling to new parents successful settings *steer* parents to the less popular days.

Alternatively, successful settings ensure that their most popular days have the greatest revenue by ensuring that they are not used for *Free Entitlement*.

Instead, *Free Entitlement* hours are focused on those days with less demand to protect revenue on busy days and bolster enrolment on less busy days.

This gives setting owners a unique set of choices. Either charge a premium for those parents who want Wednesdays and a discount for those who want Fridays and Mondays. Or alternatively, don't offer *Free Entitlement* on your busy days and do offer it on your least busy days. Either way, it's a win all-around and gives parents a choice.

CONCLUSION

Pricing is a key part of how you position your business. New customers will determine how they feel about the quality of your setting based on your price. Therefore, you should consider your pricing policy as part of your marketing strategy and look at it in conjunction with how it affects your profitability.

Nearly all businesses underestimate the impact of a price increase on their profitability.

Given that there are no additional costs, a price increase can impact the profit of your setting quickly and easily. Even if you deduct the hours paid for by Local Authorities, or use that as a part payment by adding additional services, this still offers significant potential for every setting.

Successful settings rarely fear price increases. They are confident that the value they provide exceeds the fees they charge parents, and therefore, fee increases become a standard process, which occurs in a structured manner and pre-determined frequency.

Successful settings also recognise that there is a huge opportunity in variable pricing. Identify how you can incentivise parents to even out weekly and annual peaks and troughs by using variable pricing and use this to strategically position your free entitlement hours in the most advantageous way.

When determining pricing think about your total revenue against your total costs and think about how you maximise revenue as a whole, and *not* as an hourly rate.

KEY POINTS

Use pricing as part of your Marketing Strategy to position your business consider:

- Your need to achieve your profit goal as discussed in *Chapter 7.*
- Your need to maximise your occupancy.
- Have a system for determining price increases, and stick to it. Do not be apprehensive to increase prices.
- Determine how you can exploit variable pricing to maximise your profitability.
- Use it to ensure that your most popular sessions generate the most revenue (i.e. never are used for *Free Entitlement*).

Al's Rant

Within the UK, with the fixed nature of fees coming from Local Authorities, many settings choose not take the opportunity to increase fees elsewhere. Despite the furore in the media, Early Years education is vastly under-priced for the amazing level of skill and care delivered by passionate staff, and when compared against primary education. In many areas too many setting positions themselves at the lower end of the market. Settings also employ a large number of very talented staff, who are often poorly paid. Settings should raise prices where ever possible to increase their profitability and better reward staff. Dog walkers often get paid more per hour than L3 qualified staff who educate the next generation. That can't be right!

CHAPTER 9: STAFF ENGAGEMENT

"Highly engaged employees make the customer experience. Disengaged employees break it." Timothy R. Clark

The *Parenta Childcare Providers Survey* highlighted that staff engagement and staff management were the biggest issues facing childcare providers, and so this chapter is focused on highlighting how successful businesses address this challenge.

Key Finding

Successful settings invest heavily in staff engagement. They recognise that having engaged staff creates an environment for enhanced customer experiences, and increased staff loyalty. They understand that staff engagement is essential for enhanced levels of success and profitability. Above all, however, they completely understand how damaging disengaged staff are, and resolve to not allow such behaviour to undermine what they are trying to achieve.

- Do you have high staff turnover in your setting?
- Are all of your staff fully engaged?
- Are all of your staff team players?
- How do you ensure that all of your staff are engaged with parents as well as the children?

STAFF ENGAGEMENT BEATS EVERYTHING

In the seminal book, *The Advantage: Why Organisational Health Trumps Everything Else,* Patrick Lencioni talks about *Organisational Health*. He states:

> *"The single greatest advantage any company can achieve is organisational health. Yet it is ignored by most leaders even though it is simple, free and available to anyone who wants it."*

Lencioni reveals that a Healthy company has the following ingredients embedded into its DNA.

- Minimal Politics
- Minimal Confusion
- High Morale
- High Productivity
- Low Turnover of staff.

Are these traits visible in your setting?

Creating a culture which embraces these attributes requires effort and understanding and yet the results are significant, especially to the bottom line.

Introducing values is the first part of defining your own bespoke culture and we've talked about this earlier.

The next set of sections are designed to challenge your thinking further, so you too can create a Healthy (or Healthier) culture within your business.

And this all starts with employee engagement.

EMPLOYEE ENGAGEMENT: THE STATISTICS

So before we start talking about employee engagement, let's talk about the statistics. They are pretty staggering!

In 2013, *Gallup* undertook a study into employee engagement. The *2013 Gallup Engagement Report* identified the categories:

- **Engaged employees** work with passion and feel a profound connection to their company. They drive innovation and move the organisation forward.
- **Non-Engaged employees** are essentially *checked out*. They're sleepwalking through their workday, putting time — but not energy or passion — into their work.
- **Actively Disengaged employees** aren't just unhappy at work; they're busy acting out their unhappiness. Every day, these workers undermine what their engaged co-workers accomplish.

And so, globally, the report says that:

- 13% of all employees are *engaged*
- 63% are *not engaged*
- 24% are *actively disengaged.*

If we narrow this down to the UK, then the results are:

- 17% engaged
- 57% not engaged
- 26% actively disengaged.

UK Staff Engagement

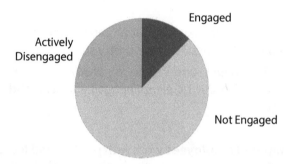

Let's start with the good news.

In an average nursery with 25 staff, four or five of them are completely engaged. They are completely inspired to deliver great care and education. They actively support you and what you are doing.

The bad news is in a similar sized setting, six or seven of your staff are so disgruntled they are actively and openly negative about the business.

And this attitude will be obvious to your customers.

Worse still, 14 of your staff really couldn't care; they are there simply because they have to be. Depressing isn't it?

These conclusions are stark.

As a country, as entrepreneurs and employers, we are collectively not doing enough to ensure that our staff are sufficiently engaged to deliver the level of service we expect and our customers demand.

Now I know that you'll think that the staff working for you are better than this survey suggests, and indeed everyone I talk to says the same. The question is, how do you know?

Your gut instinct is already telling you about a couple of people in your organisation that aren't delivering the best and most enthusiastic service to parents, and I suspect, like most of us (me included), we tend to ignore this knowing that replacing any member of staff is a difficult and costly exercise. It also causes significant disruption.

However, if these people are, in reality, actively damaging your business, then it's time to think again.

The key is, if you have more than about ten members of staff, you need to measure engagement to understand how you can improve it.

MEASURING STAFF ENGAGEMENT

In producing this study *Gallup* asked a sequence of questions that have come to be known as the *Gallup Q12*. The answers to these questions allow *Gallup* to identify who is and who is not engaged.

Unfortunately, due to copyright law, I am unable to reproduce these questions, though you can find out more by following this link.

https://q12.gallup.com/public/en-us/Features.

Another company has done very similar work however, and translated the questions into the following.

1. My performance is measured against outcomes and metrics that are clearly explained.
2. I have access to everything I need in order to perform well at my job.
3. My strengths are recognised here and I put them into practise every day in my job.
4. I regularly receive meaningful recognition for doing my job well.
5. I am happy with my relationship with my manager and I know that someone at works cares about me.
6. My manager supports me to get even better at the skills I'm valued for here.
7. My opinions are taken into account and considered here.

8. The vision or mission of the organisation is clearly defined and my job is important to achieve it.
9. My colleagues are committed and accountable for doing quality work.
10. At work, I consider one of my co-workers to be a true friend.
11. My personal progress and development is important to my manager and the company.
12. In my role, there are ongoing opportunities to learn and grow.

As you reflect on these questions, ask yourself truthfully how your staff would respond.

In my own experience, there were certain enlightening elements which I, and my more senior staff, were not undertaking sufficiently.

And therein lies the amazingly powerful nature of this study. As you examine the questions in detail, you can break them down into their constituent parts.

Q1.   I have a clear job description and clear objectives.
Q2.   I have the right resources.
Q3.   I am offered professional development opportunities.
Q4.   I am given feedback.
Q5.   I am given feedback.
Q6.   I am given feedback.
Q7   I am given feedback.
Q8.   My work is meaningful to me.
Q9.   The work I do is quality.
Q10. Relationships at work are positive.
Q11. I am given feedback.
Q12   I am offered professional development opportunities.

When you look at these question, you realise that five of the 12 questions are about feedback, two of them are about professional development, one about having objectives, two about quality meaningful work, one about a positivity and the final one about having the right tools.

The feedback issue is easy to solve and free, as are the ones about having objectives, meaningful work, and positivity. And in most cases, especially in England, much professional development is also free.

So there really is an opportunity for everyone to quickly, easily, effectively and freely, boost staff engagement.

The next question is, are you willing to start surveying your own staff to identify where you need to improve?

By doing so, you'll be able to keep identifying the areas you need to improve in order to move more of your staff into the *Actively Engaged* category.

Engaged staff are the ones your customers respond warmly to, and who will ultimately ensure the long-term success of your childcare business.

These are the staff you will rely on, who always go the extra mile and who will be with you for a very long time. Psychologically, these are your high performers who drive the success of the business.

Conversely, those who are actively disengaged are the ones who are busy undermining your work. They are there because they have to be, not because they want to be. They will be paying lip-service to you whilst undermining the goals you are trying to achieve.

These people bring the team down by constantly quipping, and moaning about how bad things are. They believe that the grass is greener on the other side and so the level of service and commitment to your customers suffers.

If you have high staff turnover, this is sure fire proof that you are not ensuring that your staff are actively engaged. You need to work on changing it.

To change engagement you need to ensure your staff

know where you're going and clearly understand your values (as outlined in *Chapter 1*). They need to know you value their work and that you see opportunities for them to develop. They need to know you care.

Beyond that, they need to know the journey they're on. We talked about the need to articulate your vision; your *journey*. Do your staff know, share and embrace your journey?

BACK TO VISION

Childcare companies that unite their people to their purpose operate differently from those who don't. It's back to *Vision* and WHY. Leaders of these companies hire, market, reward and develop differently.

Vision extends externally from your organisation too. In the study *Follow this Path: How the World's Greatest Organisations Unleash Human Potential,* authors Coffman and Gonzalez-Molina studied millions of employees and customers and conclude that emotional engagement is the *fuel* that drives productive employees and profitable customers.

The first two steps on the path to greatness are:

- Acknowledge the role that emotion plays in driving business outcomes.
- Acknowledge that all employees possess innate talents that can be emotionally engaged.

Why is this relevant to your setting?

Because in countless childcare establishments I've toured there are staff who are clearly disengaged. And now you know the statistics from *Gallup* on disengagement, it's likely that you, too, have an issue to address.

Verify the level of disengagement for yourself. Is your staff turnover a source of frustration?

Remember this was the largest area of concern amongst providers in our study.

In *Built to Last*, Porras proves that a strong foundational vision and values statement is a key driver of long-term success.

Start by defining your Vision, Why and core values as explained in *Chapter 2*.

According to Porras' work, companies that operate without a Vision tend to have:

- Constant changes in direction.
- Erratic financial results.
- High staff turnover.
- Loss of key leadership every few years.
- Customer complaints.
- Employee dissatisfaction.

THE POWER OF WE

We talked about building trust and communication and creating an open atmosphere. A key tenant of building trust is moving from *us and them*, to *we*.

As I walk around childcare settings *silos* are all too visible. This is where staff work in small groups and consider their own needs, not the needs of the whole team. *Silo-ism* is incredibly hard to battle, but must be worked on and overcome.

Do this by changing your culture to *we*.

- We have to ...
- We will ...
- We achieved ...

We changes the dynamic. With *we* it's *our* problem and *our* success, not *your* problem or *your* success.

Practising *we* is hard, but it's a culture shift that must embraced. When your team becomes *we* everyone wins. The *them and us* disappears as does the *that's not my job mentality*. Instead, it becomes how *we* solve that issue today.

STAFF REVIEWS

In the past, many companies undertook staff reviews *annually*. Today, more enlightened companies review their staff *quarterly*.

Reviewing staff annually has little effect on their performance. If the member of staff hasn't been operating at their best or doesn't understand something, you'll have been allowing them to continue in this manner for far too long.

Although it takes effort and commitment on your part, quarterly reviews are the way to ensure that your staff members are progressing well in their jobs and living by your values.

Reviews need to be two-way.

Staff should have an opportunity to advise you in writing in advance of the review what's working well and what isn't, and you'll need time to digest this information and ensure you are able to tackle the key points.

Within the review, you should set *SMART Targets* or *Objectives* for the member of staff so they have absolute clarity on what is expected of them. Remember, people will behave how you measure them, so drive the behaviours and deliverables that you want by making these part of the review.

You may already know that SMART stands for *Specific, Measurable, Achievable, Realistic* and *Time-bound*. If your targets aren't SMART, then they are not sufficiently robust.

INTERNAL COMMS

If you have a single site setting and less than a dozen or so staff, personally communicating with each member of staff is relatively easy.

As your childcare business grows, so staff engagement becomes increasingly difficult. Ensuring that everyone knows what's going on and stopping the inevitable rumour mill must become an increased priority for you.

You will need a system to ensure that everyone is kept informed. *Internal comms* is a key element for ensuring that all your staff know how the business is progressing and what is working and what isn't.

Usually, this is an email or printed newsletter. Whichever form you chose to use, ensure that staff receive an update at least monthly.

A really effective alternative, though, is a closed *Facebook* group. A closed *Facebook* group is a brilliant mechanism for communicating with all of your staff. Almost all of your staff will have a *Facebook App* on their smartphones, irrespective of their age. They will also be used to checking it daily.

A closed group allows you to take advantage of the functionality of *Facebook*, but while only being visible to those you have invited.

We use this system at *Parenta*.

With over 140 staff and more than 60% of them home-based, we have found this to be a really effective means of creating a community and ensuring that all staff are engaged.

The quote at the beginning of *Chapter 12* is *"Tell me how you measure me, and I will tell you how I will behave."* by Eli Goldratt.

Another way of saying this is: *"What gets measured gets done".*

In your monthly newsletter, make sure you are reinforcing the goals you expect your staff to have achieved, and how well the team is performing in achieving those goals.

Once you have set your goals with your key people, constantly communicate with them to build trust, track progress of the goal, and give feedback they can relate to.

RECOGNIZE

Recognition of staff achievement is another powerful tool that is often underutilised. Ensure staff know they are making great headway within their role by telling them, and give encouragement and compliments.

Equally, talk positively about the achievements of the company as a whole. If you're going through a difficult patch (we all do) ensure that you talk about how much better things will look as soon as you get through it.

CELEBRATE SUCCESS

As we have discussed, staff engagement is critical to the success of your business. We have talked about measuring staff engagement, and about the importance of quarterly staff reviews and communication with staff.

The last piece of the staff engagement strategy is to ensure that success is celebrated.

We talked about the need to determine a set of values for your staff to work by.

By celebrating the success of these values you reinforce their meaning into the business.

Likewise, every time any major milestone is hit, your team should celebrate their success.

So, once you have determined what the goals are for your organisation, ensure that all your staff know you have achieved them by celebrating.

Statistics prove that those companies who take the time

to celebrate success achieve far more than those who don't. The process becomes cyclical. As you achieve more, so you celebrate more. As you celebrate more, so you achieve more.

But don't wait until the final goal has been achieved to celebrate. Instead, celebrate milestones along the way. If you have a tracking dashboard as I'll explain in *Chapter 11* you will be able to see how you are progressing. Ensure your team knows that they are achieving by highlighting progress in your monthly newsletter and celebrating each step.

Sharing performance information adds to engagement.

STAFF BRANDING

The next thing to consider is how your staff *look* and *act* with parents.

Now, I know that your staff will probably be dressed in polo shirts or tabards with your branding.

But the reality is some nursery staff often look very scruffy, conveying the impression they don't really care.

Now go back to the chapter on marketing and reflect if this is the image of the exceptional experience you want to deliver.

And remember too, that as your staff walk around your community, covered in your branding, what they do, how they look and how they behave, directly impacts on the perception (and perceived quality) of your business.

As an example, I used to work relatively close to a setting run by a large major chain. They've gone bust now, so telling the story doesn't really matter. The uniform of the setting was bright yellow, with the logo in the upper right-hand corner and the name of the chain written in huge letters on the back.

The setting was on a large business park with several blue chip companies and many other offices. The dress code for the business people walking past the nursery on the daily sandwich run, was suit and tie.

So, I want you to imagine the daily trek to the local sandwich shops. In amongst all the office workers, dressed smartly, are these brightly coloured people.

Sounds positive, doesn't it?

And it would have been if the bright yellow shirts were clean and the rest of the dress was smart. Only it wasn't.

These staff members clearly came out of the setting having just provided lunch for the children. They were covered in spilt food. The uniform didn't fit. The jogging bottoms were unflattering and filthy. Shoes were often worn out. And worse of all – they were all smoking!

So, now imagine you're a successful business person walking past these nursery staff. You're just about to go on maternity leave. In several months, you'll be returning to work, and the nursery on the business park would be ideal as it's within walking distance of your office.

Whether you are a smoker or not, you don't want staff breathing smoke over your six-month-old baby. If you're about to spend a large proportion of your pay cheque on childcare, do you really think this would create a good impression of the nursery before you even stepped through the door?

This chain spent a huge amount of money on branding. I know this as a fact as we were responsible for their web-presence. And when I say huge, I mean several tens of thousands of pounds.

No matter how good the website or how amazing the facilities, the perception within the local community was poor, simply because the staff were not engaged enough to recognise the impact of how they looked and acted while wearing branded clothing.

The moral of the story is this. You'll spend a substantial amount of money on your branding. Don't destroy it, by allowing your staff to walk out of the building branded unless they are reflective of your values.

In this story, management allowed staff to portray the value of *we really don't care*. No wonder the chain went bust!

DRESS CODE

The dress code in your setting is a key part of your branding. Now I know you have your logo on the uniform, but it could be so much better and transform how your business is perceived.

In every setting, almost without exception, the staff walk around in a branded polo shirts or tabards. No issues with that. Except?

Except they are so unflattering!

Successful settings recognise that polo shirts come in different shapes and sizes. When you order your next batch, get the female versions for the girls, not the generic versions. The cost is almost identical and yet the impact is immense.

Oh, and order extra to cover the inevitable accidents.

Agree on standard trousers and footwear, and don't allow shoes that are worn out with holes in them. I see this often in settings and it looks dreadful.

Ensure uniforms are clean. Yes, I know that seems obvious; but you'll need staff to have spare pairs of everything and to be ready to change through the day when they start to get too scruffy.

What about tattoos? Some people love them, some people hate them. As in higher-end hotels, they should be covered when at work. Why? Because your values and attitudes may not align with those of your customers. You need therefore to take the most severe set of guidelines and apply them, just as they do within the police force where tattoos are not allowed on hands, necks and faces, and only allowed on arms if they remain covered.

Don't forget that a prospect is worth up to £50,000 to you, so you want them to feel comfortable with every element of how staff look.

SHOW YOUR STAFF YOU VALUE THEM

If you want your staff to deliver the best service then nothing is more important than making them feel that you value their efforts and you respect them as individuals. I know it sounds silly, but you'll be amazed at how many bosses don't thank their staff often. It's almost as if it's beneath them.

So the message is simple, make sure you thank your staff regularly for what they do, and praise them at least weekly. If you don't, staff will start to become disengaged.

And it's so simple to go a few steps further.

You know the birth date of all your staff, so send them a card, just from you, on their birthday. Oh, and slip £20 in it. If you've got 15 members of staff, this costs you £300 per year. £300 to keep your staff motivated, and to show you care and value them is a great investment, believe me!

STAFF TO PARENT ENGAGEMENT

Every member of your staff, from the shy 17-year-old upwards, must engage with parents and guests properly.

Let's just stop here to think. You intrinsically already know that when a parent leaves their child with you, they are doing so on trust. Trust that has built up during the engagement of the parent from your website, to the way you dealt with the initial enquiry and the show round.

Your staff are your key assets. Your secret weapon. You must ensure that staff engage parents with a warm smile. They should greet parents appropriately (*Hello* never *Alright?*), introduce themselves and shake hands firmly.

Just think what those few simple actions say about your professionalism. Such respectful and friendly greetings will set you apart from the competition immediately and cost precisely nothing.

The honest truth is often staff are allowed to behave in a manner that does not reflect well on the owners, and certainly, doesn't reflect the values of the setting.

It's important to note that this behaviour is rarely malicious. Staff behave in a certain way because they haven't been trained how to be better.

I was at a small setting the other day and was observing some new parents bring in their two-year-old son. Whilst the staff were friendly, the experience for the parents was poor.

This is what happened.

The parents and the child were greeted at the door by a member of staff. The parents introduced themselves and explained it was their son's first day. The member of staff replied they weren't expecting the child on that day, and had him down as starting in two weeks.

After some confusion, the mother produced a letter from the setting confirming that indeed the child was due to start on this day.

The member of staff was good! She didn't panic and calmly explained that it wasn't a problem, the child could come in any way.

She proceeded to introduce the parents to the child's keyworker who took over. The key worker was lovely and relaxed. The parents were asked to sit at a child's table where the keyworker ran through the induction paperwork.

She did so in a positive way and explained the documents for recording the child's learning journey. But there was clearly a problem. The key worker spoke so quietly the parents couldn't hear. They asked her to repeat herself time and time again.

The keyworker also forgot to explain the workings of the setting; such as where to leave bags and bottles and how the setting was structured.

The good news was the child was clearly confident, and went off to play on his own, but the service received by the parents wasn't as good as it should have been.

The reality is, mistakes can happen with bookings. But overall the impression the parents were given was the whole process was *adequate*. If there was a shiny new nursery just round the corner, I suspect the parents would have been tempted to go elsewhere.

My point is, it's too easy to be mediocre. If you want to set your childcare business apart from the competition you must ensure your induction systems are absolutely perfect. In my example, the keyworker probably has no idea how she was perceived. It is the responsibility of the nursery owner to ensure that such awkward events never happen.

And whilst we're on the subject of my visit to this particular setting, there's one other point I noted. Other than the keyworker and the lady at the door, not one other member of staff even acknowledged these new parents! Not a hello, a nod, or even a smile, let alone the more formal introductions I mentioned earlier. What a wasted opportunity to impress them and re-enforce their decision to send their child to that setting!

CONCLUSION

Successful businesses recognise that staff engagement is one of the prerequisites of business success. They ensure they measure engagement and have effective mechanisms for dealing with those staff who are not engaged. They recognise that successful internal communications are essential for staff engagement. They learn the positives from studies like the *Gallup Q12* and ensure they implement systems to maximise engagement.

Successful settings and businesses ensure they have a culture of high performance by moving the business to quarterly targets, ensuring staff reviews are undertaken quarterly and that *SMART* objectives are set which drive the business forward.

Lastly, successful settings recognise that hiring new staff has to be systematised and that it's critical to constantly recognise and reward success.

KEY POINTS

1. You must ensure that all your staff are engaged.

- Undertake regular staff surveys using the *Gallup* questions to identify the magnitude of the issue of disengagement in your setting. Don't make the mistake of assuming you don't have a problem.
- Use the Information within the *Gallup* survey to make sure there are robust feedback mechanisms to staff from you and your management team.
- Ensure you *Vision and Values* are pre-determined and available for staff to refer too. Make sure staff know their work is meaningful and why it is meaningful.

2. Always utilise the power of *we*.

- Making everything about *our* success and every comment about *we* will solve each problem.

3. Have your team run on quarterly cycles

- Ensure staff reviews are undertaken quarterly and that SMART objectives for every member of staff are set that drive the success of the business
- Ensure that you set the top-line goal and that everyone cascades this objective downwards to their staff. This way the whole company is aligned with the same objectives.

Al's Rant

There is an outstanding setting I work with in the South-East, where the staff are always, without exception, immaculately turned out.

Yes, they all wear Polo shirts, but they are exceptionally clean, hair is tidy, trousers and shoes smart.

Their spotless branded clothing and immaculately turned-out image just shouts quality. Other than the costs of extra sets of clothing, there is no cost for the owners, and yet the image in the community is exceptional. As staff walk out of the setting, they are the best advertising possible.

And it's free advertising. Are you using this type of free advertising?

CHAPTER 10: STAFF MANAGEMENT

*"Leaders are not responsible for the results.
Leaders are responsible for the people
who are responsible for the results."* Simon Sinek

Staff management was identified as a key issue in the *Parenta National Childcare Survey,* so this chapter will discuss the management of staff and how to address poor staff performance.

Key Finding

Successful managers and owners realise there has to be a distinction between themselves and staff. They understand the importance of onboarding the right staff and quickly moving on staff who are not performing or who are disengaged. They also understand the importance of having every member of staff work together as a team player.

- Do you have high staff turnover at your setting?
- Are all of your staff team players?
- Do you move staff on quickly when you know they're not performing?

TEAM PLAYERS

A few weeks ago I was having dinner with a client who is the owner of a very successful nursery. They are graded *Outstanding* and are making very healthy returns.

The owner was explaining how he has created an outcome-based incentive policy and how well it was driving not only staff performance but also making staff pull together.

However there is one member of staff, he lamented, who wanted the rewards, and who in all respects was a committed and talented member of staff, and yet didn't want to be involved in any of the team work. He sought my advice on what to do with this person.

In answer, I relayed the story from Clive Woodward from his autobiography *Winning!* which is the story of how he took the England team to win the *Rugby World Cup* in 2003.

The book tells how Woodward took his entire team to train with the Royal Marines on Dartmoor, some months before the *World Cup*.

At the end of the training, Woodward asked the Sergeant in charge what he thought of the team. The Sergeant replied with the expected platitudes confirming how fit and ready and motivated the team was for the forthcoming challenges.

As Woodward was leaving, however, almost as a throwaway line, the Sergeant commented that there were some in the team that he wouldn't want to go into battle with, though.

This stopped Woodward in his tracks and he sought clarification.

The Sergeant explained that when entering a hostile situation, his primary concern was the safety of his team and to this end he needed everyone to be a team player. There was no room for those focused on their own glory who didn't put the team first at all times. He believed there were a few members of the England team who fitted this self-centred description.

This gave Woodward a real dilemma.

Some of the players highlighted were his top performers, and yet he had been told explicitly by an experienced and highly-trained team-leader that he wouldn't want them on his team.

Woodward agonised for several weeks and eventually came to the inevitable conclusion. He simply could not jeopardise the success of the whole England team for these few, and consequently, they were de-selected. A brave decision as this included many star players.

And so back to my conversation with the successful nursery owner. My advice to him was exactly the same, no matter how good his member of staff was, if they were not a team player then he had no real option, but to move them on.

Within *Parenta* we took this concept to an extreme level a few years ago. We decided to remove all of the non team players from our business. We used a variety of methods and ended up removing about 20% of our staff, which at the time equated to about 20 people.

Morale in the business plummeted for two or three days.

But then it soared and the company has been growing successfully ever since.

Never underestimate how much damage non-team players and disengaged staff are doing to your business. No-one is more important than the success of the whole business.

SOLVING THE INHERENT
STAFF VS MANAGEMENT CONFLICT

Few people ever want to admit that the relationship between employer and employee in inherently adversarial.

It's adversarial because the agendas of both parties rarely align. Yes, in most cases both parties are interested in caring for and developing children, but often that's where the similarities end.

Your agenda may be on growth, increasing profit or increasing enrolment, or maybe on just meeting payroll this month. This is not the agenda for your staff. Some may be concentrating on 100 other things from hassles at home to what's happening this weekend and who's going to win the *X-Factor*.

That said, there are ways to alleviate the conflict and to yield a more positive outcome. Profit shares are one example and another is to turn the company into a partnership so that everyone is more inclined to pull together and solve problems collectively as every single person gains from the result.

At *Parenta* will are in the process of making all of our staff partners in the business. This has some significant advantages, which we are able to share with staff to create a massive *win/win*. It doesn't change the overall ownership structure, but it does allow everyone to be part of the success of the business.

If you would like to know more about our experiences with introducing a partnership, how they work and the advantages of this structure please contact me.

PAY FOR PERFORMANCE

There is also a flaw in how we traditionally reward staff.

We all pay a fixed wage for a fixed number of hours. Wages are based on the number of hours that staff work, not on their output.

Successful business owners spin this concept, to better reward staff. Firstly, they move-on those who expect pay for turning up. They are not interested in complacent staff. They simply recruit others with the motivation and ability to impact the businesses success.

They then introduce incentives that drive performance towards their objectives, thereby incentivising the behaviours they want to encourage.

There are several successful settings I work with who do

this superbly and have managed to drive individuals to focus on key tasks and behaviours. As a result, their businesses are thriving.

HIRE SLOW - FIRE FAST

Hire Slow and Fire Fast was first used by Chuck Sekeres, the founder of the successful US company *Physicians Weight Loss Centers*. His motto is profound and extremely relevant.

In *hiring slowly*, Sekeres meant hiring *thoughtfully*. And if you use this approach, you quickly realise the validity of the phrase. Problems occur when settings are desperate to find a new member of staff to maintain ratios.

Hiring thoughtfully allows settings to:

- Avoid bringing the wrong candidates into the setting.
- Ensure that candidates thoroughly fit your culture and can adhere to and promote your values.
- Ensure you're offering the right package of money and hours that really fit the need of your setting.
- Ensure the candidate can fit with your existing team.

You should *fire fast* because:

- You are probably already too late. As soon as you realise that someone is not a good fit, you need to take action.
- Everyone else will know there's a problem and are wondering why you haven't dealt with it.
- Parents want their children looked after by the best staff. If there's a problem they probably know it too.
- A disengaged member of staff will be poisoning the team and undermining you.
- Your team is only as strong as its weakest link. That weakest link is preventing the team from progressing.

Now, I know this sounds a little idealistic, when you still need to have staff to be in-ratio tomorrow. The point remains though that if a member of staff is disengaged then they are doing more harm than good. Find a replacement quickly and move them on!

HIRING

Of all the tasks I have to do within my business, hiring is the thing I dread.

Not because I don't want to add new staff to the team, I do. In fact, I relish bringing in new staff and explaining our values and my expectations of them one-to-one.

No, I dislike hiring as it's the hardest thing to get right.

Let's be honest, a 30-minute interview and a CV never provides sufficient insight into a candidate. All too often it takes several months, perhaps even years to recognise that the performance is not where it needs to be.

One of the UK's leading authorities on interviews, Professor Clive Fletcher of London University explains it succinctly, *"The Interview is easy to do, and even easier to do badly."*

Let's look at some facts about interviews:

- Extensive research carried out over more than half a century shows that an interview is a poor tool in predicting behaviour and success in the job.
- The traditional interview is only considered 5% better than pure guesswork.

All too often in Childcare, there is immense pressure to take on someone quickly.

Just thinking of the cost of bank or temporary staff is enough to give most Childcare owners nightmares.

Getting the interview wrong and employing an unsuitable person is massively costly. The *Chartered Institute of Personnel and Development* estimates the cost can reach twice the annual salary for the job. On top of that is the time wasted and the disruption caused to the business in having to start the recruitment procedure over again once it becomes clear that the wrong person was chosen in the first place.

We all tell candidates to prepare well for an interview, and yet few business owners prepare themselves for an interview. You need a robust hiring process if you want to hire the best.

Successful settings create a recruitment system that achieves the following:

- Creates high barriers to entry.
- Enforces high accountability.

It is a common mistake to consider hiring an art; it's not, it's a science.

When looking at a candidate ask, "Is this the type of person you want?" Remember the importance of engagement with children and parents and the need for team players.

So if you want engaging staff who are team players recruit with this in mind.

Successful settings start by defining the attributes they would expect from someone within their high performing team.

Consider in advance:

- What are the personal qualities you are looking for?
- What would make a candidate special?
- Are they smartly dressed (and this doesn't mean a suit, you can be in a t-shirt and still look smart)
- How did they interact with you?
- How did they make you feel?

The last one is the most important. It's a given that many nursery staff are shy, but if they can't look you in the eye during an interview, it seems unlikely they'll be able to provide the level of service to your parents that you should be demanding.

Equally, give consideration to the personalities of your current team. There's no point bringing in someone you know is likely to clash with colleagues.

Interviews should always be undertaken by at least two and never more than four people. Two because different people see and hear different things. Never more than four because that's too intimidating for the candidate.

In advance, determine a sequence of questions to ask the candidate and stick with it. All the interviewers should score the way each candidate answers each question and then sum those numbers to give a score per candidate.

Once you have seen all the candidates, check which candidates had the highest scores. These are the ones to second interview. Second interview no more than three candidates.

For the second interview, ideally, have a different member of staff with you. Go through the same process but this time, make the questions more about attitude than skill set.

Score final candidates against your values.

If you had two second interview candidates, give the best candidate a *2* for each value they excelled at, and a *1* to the candidate who was second best. If it's three candidates, it's *3* for the best, *2* for the second best and *1* for the least.

Again, add the scores together and the best candidate should be very clear to you.

The value of this system is it takes the guesswork and emotion out of selection. This more scientific approach allows settings to make a selection based on the combined views of several people, based on the skill set scores and personality traits you want.

It removes the traditional *gut-feel* approach.

MOVING STAFF ON

So if staff are disengaged, or not performing, or not team players, what should you do? Remember, if they are disengaged, they are almost certainly damaging your business, whether maliciously or not. They won't be living up to your values or practising your customer experience ethos.

The bad news is, in many cases the ship has sailed and there is little you can do to re-engage them. Keeping them on the team will allow them to continue to undermine your values. As painful as this may be, you have to move them on.

I personally never understood the importance of this until recently. I have a business mentor who coaches me, and some things he says are hard to hear. But many of his observations are profound.

He frequently says, *"It's your job to bring in the best staff you can afford. And it's your job to move them on if they're not performing".*

I have found it all too easy to procrastinate over making the tough decisions to move people on. My advice to you then is, if your gut is telling you that members of your staff are not delivering the results or service you demand, you should accept the short-term pain in order to move the business forward. I know it's difficult, but it's your responsibility. Remember, if they are disengaged, they are almost certainly negatively influencing other staff.

The problem for most setting owners is they don't move people on quickly. Often they wait more than six months before taking action. Poorly performing staff don't cure themselves.

It's like watching a bad film. Within ten minutes you know it's going to be rubbish but for some reason you feel compelled to finish it, or is that just me?

Like the bad film, most times you know a member of staff is not working out but you tend to just procrastinate until it becomes a bigger problem.

DEALING WITH LOW PERFORMANCE

Everyone, at some point in their career will encounter those who are not performing.

I'm referring to those who are not achieving their objectives and targets. These low performers demotivate those around them and can reduce the overall productivity of the team.

There is a variety of approaches managers can take to address a poor work ethic: some confront the person directly; others take an avoidance route, hoping a co-worker will instead raise the issue with the guilty party.

One thing is well known, though, most underperformers do not recognise that they are under-achieving and rarely will they correct the behaviour themselves. Therefore, you need to manage the situation carefully and take decisive action to help them change their ways.

1. GATHER NECESSARY EVIDENCE

Before you confront the person, make sure you have firm evidence of their poor work ethic. For example, you should make a note of how many times they were late to work over the past few weeks. You could also ask the opinion of one or two trusted employees in your team.

2. CLEARLY OUTLINE EXPECTATIONS

When you take on someone new, job expectations and responsibilities are not always clearly understood. When you have a private chat with the person concerned, ask them if there is any part of the job they do not understand what is expected of them. Give them the opportunity to ask questions and iron out any potential areas of confusion.

3. FIND OUT THE REASON FOR THEM UNDER-PERFORMING

The key to successfully managing a low performer is to know their background. They might be having a tough time at home, or been given some bad news recently about a family member. Sit them down and try to get to the root cause of their behaviour. If low productivity is unusual for the person concerned, it may just be a passing phase.

Try to be compassionate if the situation calls for it, but also know there is a limit and that the person still has a job to do.

4. KNOW WHAT MOTIVATES THEM

Do you know what encourages your team members to perform well? Perhaps you should? Bringing in treats to the staff room, or just offering verbal praise can work wonders to motivate your team, but if the person concerned wants more responsibility, then these rewards will not change their behaviour. Find out exactly what would encourage their best performance and then advise them what specific action they need to take to make their desires a reality.

5. MAKE THEM UNDERSTAND THE IMPACT

Nobody wants to hear they are letting down their team. One important way to highlight the poor work performance of the person concerned is to let them know the negative impact it is having on the people around them, and the effect on the nursery overall. Sometimes, this is all you need to do to make the low performer change their ways.

6. PUT THEM ON NOTICE

If you have exhausted steps 1-5 and still not seen any improvement in behaviour, it may be time for some tough love. Putting the low performer on notice can be a very effective way to drive change. During the notice period, make sure you agree on a plan of action and have regular reviews to document their progress.

7. CLEAR THE DEADWOOD

Sometimes, enough is enough. When someone has had their second (and even, third!) chance to change their work ethic and have stayed the same; it's time to clear out the deadwood. I know this sounds harsh, but it does need to happen. Childcare settings rely on the hard work, passion and productivity of their staff so, sometimes, the best thing you can do is find a new staff member.

8. DO IT WITH TOTAL INTEGRITY

It goes without saying, play by the book, stick to the rules and seek professional employment law advice if needed.

9. LEGAL PERSPECTIVE

Understand that the staff member's poor performance could compromise your legal obligations under the various regulations that govern the sector.

You need to treat potential breaches of duty of care seriously because if it can be shown *you knew* of a staff issue but didn't act, *you* could be held accountable from a *negligence* perspective. Always seek advice from appropriate professionals in this instance.

A FINAL WORD ON FRIENDS AND FRIENDSHIP

I talk to a lot of nursery owners and managers who feel they have been personally let down by staff. And I don't mean staff not turning up, or calling in sick, or leaving to work somewhere else. It's often far more personal and often cuts very deep.

When you peel back the reasons, it's more than often that the manager and the staff member have become very close friends and then that bond is broken, through the staff member breaking a trust.

This is common with newly promoted managers who have just come from the floor and struggle to make the transition to management.

In almost every case there is a common issue. And that's friendship. Having staff as friends doesn't work.

In fact, it should be even more blatant. Your staff are not your friends. They are employees.

I am not suggesting you shouldn't be friendly to staff and have fun, and enjoy their company, recognise birthdays and anniversaries, celebrate births and marriages and mourn deaths and divorces (or celebrate divorces depending on the case) but having them as close personal friends, all too often, becomes a problem.

How do you conduct a review with a close personal friend? How do you reprimand them? Worse, how do you fire them, if something dreadful happens?

Successful business owners recognise that there has to be a gap between themselves and their staff.

I repeat, this does not preclude being friendly, but successful business owners understand that there is a difference between friendly and friendship. They are not the same.

CONCLUSION

Successful settings also align the success of the business with the needs of the staff. They often do this by having profit shares, or incentive schemes, which align to company goals and reward those who achieve.

They also recognise that not all staff are right for their business and if so, proactively decide to move them on. They appreciate that this is not only best for the business but often best for the staff member too.

Successful nursery owners know they have to distinguish between friends and friendship with their staff. They also know the importance of taking their time to recruit new staff.

Lastly, leaders ensure that every member of staff is a team player. Having made that decision, they recognise that those who are not team players have no business being on the team.

KEY POINTS

1. **Aligning the goals of yourself and your staff has a huge impact on the business.** Create either a profit share scheme or a partnership, or align staff remuneration packages with specific action to achieve your goals.

2. **Bite the bullet and recognise that if you want a high performing team you must remove those staff who are not performing,** who are negative or who are not team players IF you can't turn them around.

3. **Hire slow and fire fast.** Despite the pressures of needing staff urgently, you need to ensure that you recruit staff who can see your vision and can deliver your values. Equally, when staff are not performing you need to take action and not, as most of us do, believe that things will change if you give them just a little longer. *They won't.*

4. Be very wary of allowing staff to become close, personal, friends.

Al's rant

We work in a sector where our greatest cost for our businesses is staff. It's a people sector, all about looking after, people, albeit little people. The importance of getting everyone pulling in the same direction is often overlooked. Everyone talks of team, though few are able to create a truly cohesive team within their company. When it does happen though, amazing things follow, and success and profitability increase. Every time I discuss this with setting owners I hear the issues they face with recruitment and the costs involved in bank staff whilst they seek replacements. These arguments are clearly important, and totally valid. If you want to make a difference to how your setting performs though, you are going to have to suffer some short term pain.

CHAPTER 11: MEASURING SUCCESS

*"Tell me how you measure me,
and I will tell you how I will behave".* Eli Goldratt

Within the annual *Parenta National Childcare Survey*, we asked what metrics settings use to measure their success. A clear picture emerged. Those who had comprehensive systems to collect and measure progress were more successful and more profitable. More importantly, they were tracking these metrics and trending them so they could see variations and act on this vital information.

KEY FINDING

Successful settings measure, track, and monitor key trend metrics. They use management dashboards, or spreadsheets to visualise how each metric varies over time and understand that whatever gets measured improves.

- What do you measure at your setting?
- What metrics are important to you?
- How do you know if the business is succeeding?
- How often do you review management accounts?

These questions are important as our surveys suggest that the most successful settings measure specific metrics within the business very closely.

GET READY TO MEASURE

As you go through the journey of business improvement, you need to measure key business metrics.

The theory of re-enforcement claims that whatever you focus on you get more of. So as you focus on key metrics they tend to improve because of that attention. *'What gets measured gets treasured'* is very true.

In measuring key metrics, and trending them within a *dashboard*, you will be able to track what works well against what doesn't. Inevitably, some of the advice in this book will have a bigger impact than others. You will only know if you keep track of every trend.

How frequently should you measure? That depends on what's most important. If marketing is important because your occupancy rate is down, I'd track all of your marketing funnel metrics weekly, and sum the results for monthly figures. That way you can see how your work impacts these numbers.

At *Parenta*, I track all marketing and sales metrics weekly and review these with the relevant teams. A key part of our business though is project management, and I check this every single day to identify where I need to concentrate my attention if we fall behind. So the answer is to check your progress as often as is necessary to drive your business, but never less than monthly.

And don't forget you can measure both tangible results (such as occupancy or revenues) as well as intangible results (such as customer satisfaction or staff engagement). They both have meaning as you trend them to see how you are improving.

WHAT METRICS SHOULD YOU TRACK?

The following metrics should be tracked at least monthly.

FINANCIALS

- **Revenue:** A track of total revenue (total income) is vitally important. It allows you to see variations in seasonality and whether the business is growing or declining. As you implement the strategies in this book, you should start to see revenue increasing.

- **Net Profit:** Net profit tells you that you are being successful (or not). If this is declining you need to address aspects of your business to either increase revenue (sales) or decrease costs.

- **Operating expenses:** You should be tracking your operating expenses (costs) and viewing how these change over time. Your largest cost will undoubtedly be staffing and, therefore, it's important to see how this varies as you increase your revenue.

- **Cash flow:** You will need to monitor how cash moves in and out of your business.

- **Aged debt:** Use the aged debt report from your management software to monitor the amount of debt you have older than 30 days, in pounds.
  This has a very real and tangible cost to you as defined in *Chapter 6*, so ensure you are utilising the points made to reduce this figure. If the figure starts to go up, you will need to address it urgently by implementing your late payment processes. The most successful nurseries never procrastinate on aged debt.

Marketing

- **Enquiry Lead source:** Where did your enquiry hear about you? This is a critical metric to measure, as it tells you which elements of your marketing are working.

- **Number of Enquiries:** The purpose of *Chapter 3* is to increase your number of enquiries until you are completely full. Tracking the number of *Enquiries* is, therefore, essential.

- **Marketing Qualified Leads (MQL):** As discussed in *Chapter 3*, not all enquiries are of equal value. You should track the number of enquiries which are relevant for your business as well as the total number of enquiries. So, if you're only open until 6pm and you have enquiries for after-school care past 6 pm, this would not make it as an *MQL* but if you have lots of these enquiries it might tell you your community needs a service that is not currently being offered.

- **Number of Show Rounds:** The number of show rounds is a critical piece of data. You will need to trend how many show rounds you conduct and then look at the conversion figure to see how you need to improve this vital part of the marketing funnel.

- **Show Rounds per staff member:** If more than one person does the show rounds, record the conversion rates of each team member. It's likely that one member of staff will have a higher conversion rate than another. This is good news, as you can learn what the more successful staff member is doing right so that you can improve the process.

- **Number of New Children:** You should trend the number of new children starting at your setting, and ideally the amount of *capacity* they use.

- **Number of Left Children:** You should be trending the number of children who leave the setting each month.

- **Why Children left your setting:** You should measure the reasons why children left the setting.

With the exception of those children who move on to go to school, this is going to require some brutal honesty on your part. If you use it, you can improve the care you provide and plug any gaps.

- **Why parents chose your setting:** This is an essential element to measure as it will tell you the elements of your settings parents favour most. This could be quite enlightening if they choose something that you don't see.

OCCUPANCY

- **Total occupancy (as a percentage):** Absolutely critical. It is the main measure of success for the business
- **Occupancy Wastage, in pounds (£):** This is a really important measurement as it highlights how much capacity is wasted.

STAFF ENGAGEMENT

- **Staff Engagement:** This is more difficult than other factors to implement. Measuring the *Gallup Q12* really does provide insight into how well you are performing as a leader, rather than a manager.
- **Staff Turnover:** You need to measure how many staff you lose. This tells you how much you have invested into the health of your business, and how successful your recruitment and staff engagement strategies are.

YOUR DASHBOARD

Inside your car you have a dashboard that provides you with an array of information about how your car is operating. As well as speed, your dashboard shows how much fuel you have left, the outside temperature, the oil pressure or the charge in the battery. It tells you if the lights are on and if you're using main beam or fog lights.

It gives you an instant summary of all the key elements of the operation of your car in one place, in an easy to understand lay-out.

Now, wouldn't it be great if you could have the same vital information about your business displayed in the same way?

The answer here is not only that you *could*, but also that you *should*.

A *business dashboard* provides vital information about the health of your business. It tells you what's working well and shows the areas of your business that need your attention.

Most importantly, it allows you to validate that the changes you implement are having the desired effect, enabling you to change course if any tweaks are not yielding the results you expect.

It is an invaluable addition to the successful management of your business.

And the good news? Creating such a dashboard is easy!

Determine what you want to measure, (my list would be a good starting point) and see how far back you can go with data. The further back, the more valuable the information display will be.

If you haven't tracked the information, then aim to start immediately. Create a simple sheet within *Excel,* with the months at the top starting from as far back as possible.

Then add the metrics you want to track.

I personally prefer graphs to numbers for understanding my business. It gives me an instant and very clear perspective of how things are progressing. *Parenta's* software gives a full dashboard containing these vital metrics.

BE CAREFUL - METRICS CAN LIE!

One word of caution before you barrel forward! Metrics can lie.

As an example, unless you have a very large waiting list, your occupancy is likely to fall in the summer as children moving up to for their next step leave you. August then becomes a lower occupancy month, and often recruitment is at a peak in September.

If we use a traditional method of tracking occupancy, we'd see a dip in numbers in August and a corresponding peak in September.

What would happen if you launched a new marketing promotion for September? The increase in new placements could fool you into thinking your new promotion was working. However, it could be just the normal September bubble. You could end up spending more money on a campaign that's not working; you simply wouldn't know for sure.

Using the trailing 12-month method discussed in *Chapter 7* avoids this problem. We talked about this method for revenues and profits, but it should be used for all analysis.

Whilst it sounds complicated, this is an extremely easy graph to create and even easier to read.

Add together the results of previous 12 months worth of data to create a single figure.

Next month, do the same, but this time, we'll take the 12 months back from the current month. This then gives us the sum of the previous 12 months data set and we can plot this on a graph. This is easy to do in *Excel* or *Google Docs*, and if you use *Parenta's* software it will all be done for you.

Once you have this graph based on your critical numbers, reading it is simple; if the graph shows an upward trend then this metric is doing well and you should continue.

If the graph is static, then be careful, you need to consider what's happening.

If the graph is falling, then you need to take immediate action, you have a problem.

As an example, look at the two graphs below. They represent the same data, and yet they tell completely different stories.

The line of the first graph is the real *monthly* data. Looking at the straight trend line (a trendline highlights the average position), you'd think the results are *relatively* consistent, averaging at about 100.

The second graph tells a very different story, however.

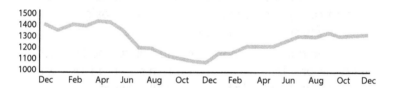

This graph shows that in the second period of 12 months to December, the numbers fell dramatically. You would not have easily determined this from the first graph. So, during the second period, June to December, the data should be cause for concern.

In the second graph, as the line starts to turn upward from January the message changes to positivity. This isn't immediately clear from the first graph.

And so I repeat. Be careful how you measure, as metrics can lie!

Of course, extending your forecasts for a further 12 months gives you a unique perspective of how the business has performed over the past 12 months, and how you expect it perform over the next 12 months.

CONCLUSION

The most successful settings, track their key metrics constantly. They measure them and trend them to see what is happening within the business.

More advanced businesses, extend this to predict outcomes over the following 12 months and are able to influence the business to achieve results.

Successful business owners in general are aware that metrics can be used to distort the truth. Rolling graphs provide a more relevant view of business than normal graphs, particularly with seasonality.

KEY POINTS

- **You must track the key metrics of your business.** Successful settings measure and monitor key metrics throughout their business in easy to update dashboards which display, at a glance, how the business is performing. These dashboards trend the results to highlight the trajectory of each of the key performance indicators (KPIs).

- **Trend everything in absolute terms and using the 12-month rolling system.** The most successful settings trend their KPIs using the 12-month rolling method so they can remove seasonality from decision-making processes. You can trend your qualitative measures as well as the quantitative measures.

- **Keep a keen eye on the metrics which directly influence your results.** Settings which need to improve their performance watch their key metrics closely. They need to be able to understand both positive and negative variances so they can adjust the business accordingly.

Al's Rant

Many of the settings I have seen tend to look at their financial results annually, when they get them from their accountants. Results are not just annual, they are constant.

Profit and loss, and all the Key Performance Indicators of the business should be checked at least every month.

Trending the results enables you to identify which KPIs need more of your attention.

Not using a dashboard system to trend your results makes it increasingly difficult to drive success. You wouldn't drive your car without one, so why drive your business without one?

CHAPTER 12: PUTTING IT ALL TOGETHER

"I believe in benevolent dictatorships,
provided I am the dictator." Richard Branson.

The clear impression that emerges from the *Parenta National Childcare Survey,* is that many providers are worried about their businesses. Much of their concerns relate to the ever changing operational conditions enforced by Government or Government agencies.

There is also a concern about financial viability from exhausted owners, constantly fighting to be profitable and improve their business.

Many will say that the profitability dilemma is down to Government Policy, though the most successful settings accept that they have to work within this framework and adapt their businesses to suit through the introduction of additional services.

In adapting their business they exploit each and every loophole within any framework guidance. Beyond that, they focus on what they can control and learn to live with what they can't.

> **Key Finding**
>
> Successful nurseries adapt their businesses to the things they can control, and this includes identifying loopholes in statutory guidance. Those things beyond their control they accept as facts of life and move on improving what they can. They develop enhanced systems so they are empowered to work *on* the business, rather than *in* the business.

- Is your setting giving you the returns you expect?
- Are you taking a commercial salary from your business?
- Is every element of the setting systematised?

ACTION PLANS

I hope it has become clear throughout this book that all aspects of the business are interdependent on each other. Whilst you can work on any one piece of your business, you need to address all of the issues to turn the commercial side of your business into a success. As mentioned in *Chapter 1* though, focus on the weakest links first.

Within your business, you will be used to *Action Planning*. So, now it's time to *Action Plan* on your business to make it more effective.

Firstly, we want you to achieve your occupancy targets so you are full.

Then we want you to collect monies as effectively and painlessly as possible. In other words: Get paid. On time. Every time.

And then we want you to measure what works and track the success of your new results: know what works and what doesn't.

YOU NEED A BUSINESS DEVELOPMENT PLAN

A traditional and easy way of creating a business improvement plan is to start with a *SWOT analysis*. Most of you will be familiar with this term, but for those who aren't, *SWOT* stands for *Strengths, Weaknesses, Opportunities* and *Threats.*

Presented as a four-quadrant grid, a *SWOT analysis* provides a proven structure that enables you to be brutally honest with yourself to see where you need to improve.

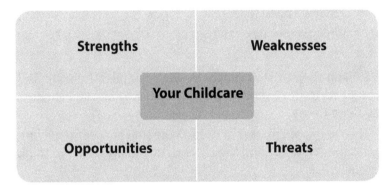

The *SWOT analysis matrix* helps you identify what you do well and what you need to improve. It allows you to see opportunities that present themselves, and any potential threats that might stand in your way.

Involve your leadership team when completing your SWOT analysis as they will have a different perspective to you, and therefore will see things differently. It's your responsibility to walk them through a detailed and thorough discussion of your *Strengths, Weaknesses, Opportunities* and *Threats* to your childcare business.

Once the *SWOT analysis* is complete, you will have a structure for your business improvement *Action Plan*. List the items you want to focus on, prioritise them, set due dates and define who is accountable.

Another way of identifying what works well and what doesn't is to allow the staff to tell you in a structured manner.

This method is similar to a *SWOT analysis*. Grab some flip-chart paper and stick the sheets around the room. This works particularly well for a new manager taking over an existing team, as the process allows everyone to share their frustrations.

Entitle the sheets:

- What works well.
- What works OK.
- What we need to fix.
- What annoys us.

Explain to your staff that you want complete honesty and you need to get everything on the table to fix the elements that don't work.

Then, hand out marker pens to all the staff and let them write what they want. During the process, encourage them to think laterally. Ask:

- What are we missing?
- What are we doing wrong?
- What could we do better?
- What are we pretending not to know?

Allow staff to take as much time as they need, and keep encouraging them to be honest. And then prepare yourself for some not-so-nice conversations as they raise issues which will be difficult to hear. The key is not to be defensive. Just let your staff write whatever they like.

Collate the comments in the *What we need to fix* and *What annoys us* categories into a number of small projects.

You'll quickly find that even if there are about 50 comments on each sheet they boil down to 10 – 20 key items that need to be fixed.

Once you've completed the exercise, the easy bit comes next. You simply need to prioritise the items or projects identified and get on with fixing them.

The good news is most of them will be procedural, and by changing your system or process you can get some quick wins.

More importantly, this process proves to your staff you are willing and able to listen to their issues. It proves that you care about them and what frustrates them.

If you include their opinions you will get more and more buy-in from the whole team. And you'll move towards the state of *We* discussed in *Chapter 8*.

Of course, you'll need to keep meeting with the staff every month or so to update them on the progress you're making.

It's up to you to drive through the changes that you need to transform your business and to drive profitability. Remember, only by being profitable can you invest in the business and increase quality.

The most successful settings and businesses undertake this exercise every quarter which builds continuous ongoing improvement, as new issues always come up.

SYSTEMATISATION

There are a number of key tenets in this book which are talked about in context and need further examination on their own.

The most important of these is *systematisation*.

Systematisation is the creation of systems which run of their own accord, without you having to determine in advance what you need to do to address a specific issue.

And systematisation is a big deal.

Just look at some of the comments about systems from a few major business authors.

- All wealth is built on systems. – Dan Kennedy
- Let systems run the business and people run the systems. People come and go, but systems remain constant. – Michael Gerber
- For a business owner, systems set you free. – Keith Lee

As an example, let's go back to the subject of bad debt from *Chapter 6*. If you have a clear and robust process in place, which clearly defines what happens when a parent owes fees for more than 30 days, you stick to it (the *nice* verses *commercial* debate), and your parents have clarity on how it will be implemented, then when these issues occur, the process automatically should swing into action.

You shouldn't need to *think* about how to address this issue, you've already done that. You simply implement the systems which you have already devised.

And this is the case with all the issues I mentioned. By creating systems around them, they should become self-fulfilling.

Now, I'm not saying they will be perfect the first time you use them; they won't.

You'll have to learn from your implementations and refine each of your processes to ensure they are robust and yielding the correct result. But each time you refine them, things start to work better.

The trick is to translate all of the elements defined in this book into processes and systems that make life easier.

Yes, it will take time to create the processes, but it will add strength to the way your business runs. In the long-run, systemisation saves you time and effort.

Knowing exactly what to do each time an issue arises decreases the time and stress involved in making those decisions.

So let's define the term *systemisation*. As you know, a system is a pre-determined business process which, when used consistently, delivers the same result. It also allows anyone, irrespective of their experience to be able to implement a process.

Systems allow you to delegate procedures effectively, knowing that if your staff follow the defined procedures the expected result should occur.

Systemisation then is the creation of multiple systems which collectively yield the correct results when processes are followed.

Now, you will already have multiple systems dealing with the childcare side of your business. From what to do when you get the call about an inspection to dealing with the huge array of policies and procedures you need to run childcare effectively, and many will have systems that are effective within the business side, though I suspect they can be enhanced.

The most successful settings simply extend that logic into the business side of their setting, in all respects.

From the simplicity of answering the phone to prospective parents, through to the process of reviewing the performance of your staff, I'm suggesting that you need to systematise each element.

And, I know it may seem like a large amount of work to create all of these systems for your business, but you need to constantly think about the huge impact on your long-term future.

For context, most settings have *documented* emergency procedures in place. They know exactly what to do step-by-step if there's an emergency like a fire or an accident.

Some settings have one-page checklists for technical matters such as turning on and off their overnight security systems; or banking; or registering a new child.

These systems make life easier. You also do a hundred other different tasks every day. Most of your staff have received some form of *How we do things around here training* - usually verbal. These are your systems. They already exist. I'm saying start documenting them.

There is a world of operational efficiency difference between settings who have their systems documented and those that don't.

Settings that undertake this exercise notice the benefits almost immediately.

Get your staff involved. Ask them to suggest areas where systematisation would make their lives easier. Trust me, they will have good ideas!

MOVING FORWARD

I started this book by stating that according to *NDNA*, only 51% of Childcare nurseries were expected to make a profit in 2016.

I have explained strategies and tactics to improve specific elements of the business and to track how things are progressing.

While the fact that half the number of nurseries in the UK are not expected to make a profit is of grave concern, we should acknowledge the fact that half *do* expect to make a profit!

Many smaller providers believe that it's the large mega-chains that are making the money. And whilst it's true that some of them do make good returns, a significant number of them don't. Indeed, as a percentage of turnover, many smaller settings are doing far better than the mega-chains.

So, what does differentiate successful nurseries which generate enough profit to allow Childcare owners to enjoy running their businesses, from those who constantly struggle to make ends meet?

The difference is a style of management and of how they approach improving their services.

Successful Childcare owners start by creating high barriers to entry for staff into their business. They ensure that they employ the staff with the best, *can-do* attitude, who want to look smart and want to deliver an exceptional service. Jim Collins, the author of *Good to Great* describes this as getting the *right people on the bus.*

They embed this high standard into the structure of their company and use it as a foundation to create a high performing team.

They have clearly defined the WHY of their business and continuously articulate this to their staff and customers. It pervades everything they do, including all of their marketing messages as well as how they deliver an extraordinary customer experience.

Their values are explicitly defined and ingrained into how they conduct their business. They live and breathe these values and require their team to do so too.

They have clear financial controls in place, including robust payment systems, so late payments are a rare occurrence and excessive bad debt is a thing of the past.

They have deployed structured marketing systems that constantly generate new leads ensuring they are always full.

Their staff members are all engaged with parents and want to deliver an exceptional level of service.

And most importantly, they have learned what works and what doesn't through trial and error. By having a clear dashboard for tracking key metrics they quickly see when things turn the wrong way and adeptly address these issues.

It is this last aspect, the facility to constantly see how the business is performing, which gives these Childcare owners the edge.

The good news gets better! As you start your journey into making your childcare setting more profitable, things start to get easier. The old saying is: *'Success breeds success.'* In a sense, this is totally correct, as you change course on each of these elements, so it frees up your time to deal with the next.

Implementing each solution will change the nature of your business, moving it towards a smooth flowing system.

As this happens, you will be able to fret less about the commercial side of your business and focus more on the enjoyment of running a profitable Childcare setting.

PROFITABILITY

I entered the Childcare sector over 18 years ago. During that time, a lot has changed. But one of the most profound changes is the attitude to profit.

Eighteen years ago, *profit* was a dirty word spoken in hushed tones and rarely talked about openly.

It's time to stamp on this concept once and for all.

Being profitable is now absolutely essential for all Childcare providers. You simply can't continue to invest in high-quality services and staff if you're not profitable. Services to children inevitably fail if the provider doesn't focus enough attention on stemming losses.

If you're willing to accept that profitability is a prerequisite for a successful childcare provider then I want to extend the goal to achieving financial freedom.

By financial freedom, I don't mean profiteering and taking huge amounts of money from the business. I am however advocating that owner managers take *real* salaries to match the fact they are the MDs of small businesses. Far too many Childcare owners see their salary as the last element in the chain, and only to be paid if there's enough left. They often take a minimal salary to simply cover the cost of living.

This needs to be consigned to history. If you're beyond the start-up phase of your business, then it's time you took a sensible salary.

If you follow my advice you will start to see increased profitability of your business. Follow my suggestions for several months, implement the systems and focus your attention on ensuring that your dashboard is presenting you with the right data trends and your setting will start to become full and your waiting list will increase.

You are then able to revisit the pricing of your services.

When we started our journey together, your business may not have been giving *WOW!* customer service, and not engaging with customers in the way it does now.

You have therefore, moved the positioning of your business. No longer just another childcare provider in *Anytown* your facility should have a reputation for delivering an exceptional service, which far exceeds your customers' expectations.

If this is the case, then it's time to think about your family and your needs. If you have built the financial models explained in *Chapter 7*, you can now model what would happen if you put up your prices.

Now, let's be clear. I'm not suggesting that you be excessive. But I am suggesting your business should now be competing at the same level as the shiny new setting up the road.

They might have a new building, but you'll have customers raving about your service. And you should be able to move up your pricing to somewhere similar to them. The most profitable segment for any business is the top end where the service becomes aspirational as customers (parents) are willing to pay for quality.

This is the final piece of the jigsaw to improving your business. Having worked so hard to ensure your delivery is exceptional, it's time you took the rewards.

CONCLUSION

Successful settings regularly review the effective elements of the business and work with the staff to identify the elements that need further attention. They ask searching questions to spot problems and create actions plans.

Settings that undertake these reviews on a quarterly basis, often see rapid progress in achieving their goals.

Successful nursery owners understand they need systems and processes. They introduce systems at every opportunity allowing the systems to run the business so they can focus on other issues.

Lastly, but most importantly, successful nursery owners recognise that they must be profitable to deliver the highest calibre *Early Years* care, which includes a realistic, commercial equivalent reward structure for themselves as well as above industry rewards for staff.

KEY POINTS

1. The most successful settings involve staff to **create action plans to drive their business forward.** They do this on a regular basis on every element of the business. Staff involvement in determining solutions gains their buy-in.

2. Successful settings recognise that **systematisation is key to their long-term success and delivering a consistent level of service.** They have processes written for each element of their business and never fail to action them at the appropriate time.

3. The most successful settings recognise that they must **treat their business in a commercial manner to improve profitability.** In doing so they are able to invest in infrastructure and better care, as well as improved pay and conditions for staff and themselves.

Al's Rant

For many owners and managers, life in the sector is hard. Yes, they have the passion, enthusiasm and dedication to provide an outstanding level of care and education, and yet they are often paid well below market rates. When coupled with the huge risks of running a childcare setting, the rewards are often not covering the day-to-day expenses, let alone a realistic commercial salary.

And yet there are settings I work with that are making very substantial rewards. This includes small 30 or 40 place settings with around 15 staff to chains with over 700 staff.

Either way, there are owners and managers in this sector who are seeing the financial rewards of their endeavours.

And of course, this filters down through the staff, to the children.

It is absolutely possible for everyone in the sector to become profitable and successful.

I started this book with a question, and I choose to end with the same question.

'Everyone in childcare is aware of the enormous contribution that the Early Years sector makes to the children in our care, to hard-pressed working parents and to local communities, as well as to society as a whole. Imagine how much more it could contribute if every childcare business was successful?'

CHAPTER 13: HOW CAN WE HELP YOU?

Throughout the book I have mentioned *Parenta*, the company I co-founded in the year 2000, and which has now grown to incorporate over 150 staff and works with over 5,000 childcare providers.

At *Parenta* our mission is clear. We want to help *Early Years* providers to become more successful. And whether that's through our software systems, or through a vocational training apprenticeship, we exist to help providers.

Unusually, we are a partnership, with the majority of our staff partners in the business. This means they share in our success. If we have a good year, then they all earn more.

But importantly, partnership changes the dynamic of how we work. It means we are all pulling in the same direction, and all strive to make a difference to our customers.

And that doesn't mean we don't make mistakes; we do. But we work hard to ensure that such issues don't hinder our customers, and when they do, we hold our hands up and apologise.

We strive to work alongside our customers, as partners in moving the sector forward.

Everything from our positioning statement through to our products is about working together. Working together for our children is our positioning statement, and it sums up exactly how we want to work - together - with our customers.

We provide an array of services to help you.

It's not appropriate to list them all here, but we can provide everything from management software and learning tracking software, to fee collection systems and marketing systems.

On the training front we provide qualifications from Level 1 to Level 5, with funding or part funding available for many courses.

We also have a team of very experienced and successful nursery owners, who provide consultancy services to help those settings who need to move towards outstanding in everything they do.

And we provide a wealth of resources, guides and magazines, for free, on our website at *www.Parenta.com*.

If you think we can help you, just fill in a contact form on *www.Parenta.com* and one of our friendly staff will be delighted to talk you through some of our solutions.

We are here to help you.

The ParentaTrust

All profits from sales of this book will be donated to our registered charity, the *ParentaTrust*.

The *ParentaTrust* provides pre-school education for thousands of orphaned and disadvantaged children in East Africa's poorest nations.

Set-up in 2013, the *ParentaTrust* has so far opened four nursery schools in Uganda. Each school houses around 150 children, from impoverished backgrounds.

We aim to provide hope and regeneration in deprived communities across East Africa.

Throughout East Africa vulnerable children are living lives of deprivation and the greatest tragedy is their lack of education. Given the opportunity to attend school, the children develop skills to lift their families out of the poverty cycle.

These children don't want handouts, they just want a chance to help themselves! A quality education is literally a chance for survival; a lifeline where they will get an opportunity to contribute to their community and their nation's much-needed development.

The Ugandan economy is predominantly agricultural. During the 1970s and early 1980s, the Ugandan nation suffered two bloody dictatorial regimes, under Idi Amin and Milton Obote. Genocide occurred in several areas of Uganda and left many citizens living in extreme poverty, often on less than $1.25 a day.

In 1986, Uganda came under the control of President Yoweri Museveni, who introduced democratic and economic reforms, which are slowly lifting the country.

The *ParentaTrust* is well on its way to complete its mission of building ten nursery schools within ten years. In doing so, we will have provided a pre-school education for at least 1500 children, but of course, these numbers keep growing as children move beyond the nursery setting into primary school, and the next generation of infants enter our schools.

The first part of the work that the *ParentaTrust* undertakes is to build a pre-school in a deprived community. Once completed, our work isn't done. Far from it. Each child within our schools needs sponsorship, as invariably they have no-one to pay their fees, being orphans.

We need to ensure that each child is sponsored so they can attend school and benefit from an education.

The *ParentaTrust* is looking to partner with Childcare providers in the Western world to sponsor a child at one of our nurseries. To find out more visit *www.Parenta.com/charity*

CHILD SPONSORSHIP

Child sponsorship gives hope to orphaned pre-school children. It provides them with their education, with one hot meal per day, with a uniform (no shoes) and with a writing book. It costs just £17 per month per child.

Could your Childcare setting sponsor a deprived orphan child from Africa? *ParentaTrust* arranges all the details and validates that the child is in need. We provide you with an update and photos of the child every six months, along with a pack to promote your links with your African partner nursery school. It provides a unique opportunity to create a partnership with our organisation to engage your children and parents with one of our African nurseries.

It also positions your school as altruistic and able to help those whose lives are fundamentally different from our own.

The elder children in your setting can even send drawings to their African friends as we seek to build the bonds of friendship for the next generation.

To find out more about our *Child Sponsorship* packages and how your school could partner with us, please go to

www.Parenta.com/charity

From here you can find out how to partner with us, and what we can achieve together to make a difference.

EXPLORATORY VISITS

Are you curious to understand what sub-Saharan Africa is really like? Do you want to understand how pre-school education works in Africa?

The *ParentaTrust* arranges short, fact-finding visits to Uganda every year to meet with the children we sponsor, to see the buildings we have built and show UK educators how schooling works in Africa.

It also allows you to meet the hundreds of children we support in our-pre-schools.

These week-long trips encompass visits to all the *ParentaTrust* pre-schools and several other schools. You also share in the drilling of a fresh water well in a community that has never had fresh water. The experience is incredibly humbling and often life-changing.

Many people think that going to such places is tough because there will be so much sorrow. Yes, the trips are tough. There are heart-breaking stories at every turn. However, the visits are really about joy.

It is quite incredible to see the joy on children's faces as they see new schools provided for them or joy on the face of a village elder who has never had a drink of fresh water in his life!

This is the gift that *ParentaTrust* brings to these communities.

The *ParentaTrust* welcomes applications from all members of the *Early Years* Community to visit Uganda with us and see what's really happening on the ground. I assure you, you will return as an ambassador for the work we are doing.

To find out more, or to register for the next trip to Uganda, please visit *www.Parenta.com/charity.*

Alternatively, if you'd like to discuss the work of the *ParentaTrust* and how you may can help, please contact the Trustees or me via:

Email   *info@Parentatrust.org* or *allan@Parenta.com*
Twitter   *@AlPres*

I welcome the opportunity of discussing what how the charity can work with you.

The *ParentaTrust* is proud to work with *Fields of Life,* a charity from Northern Ireland that provides primary and secondary education throughout East Africa. They have built over 140 schools and sunk more than 4,000 fresh water wells. More information on *Fields of Life* is available at:

www.fieldsoflife.org

References

Reports

- *The Power of Pricing: How to make an impact on the bottom line.* (2013). PricewaterhouseCoopers LLP.
- *The Parenta National Childcare Survey.* (2015). Parenta Group Ltd.
- *Review of childcare costs: The analytical report. An economic assessment of the early education and childcare market and providers' costs.'* (2015). Department for Education. DFE-00295-2015.
- *Annual Nursery Survey, England.* (2016). National Day Nurseries Association (NDNA).

Books

- Coffman. C. and Gonzalez-Molina. G. (2004). *Follow this Path: How the World's Greatest Organisations Unleash Human Potential.* Random House Business Book.
- Collins. J. (2001). *Good to Great.* Random House Business.
- Collins. J and Porras. J. (2005). *Built to Last: Successful Habits of Visionary Companies.* Random House Business.
- Goldratt. E. (1997). *Critical Chain.* Gower Publishing Ltd.
- Goldratt. E. (2004). *The Goal: A process of ongoing improvement.* Routledge.
- Hamadache. A. (2015). *Give your guest a WOW: 21 ways to create impeccable hotel customer service that leaves a lasting impression.* Rethink Press.

- Jameson. H and Watson. M. (1997). *Starting and Running a Nursery: The Business of Early Years Care.* Nelson Thornes.

- Lencioni. P. (2012). *The Advantage: Why Organisational Health Trumps Everything Else in Business.* Wiley.

- Sinek. S. (2011). *Start with Why: How Great Leaders Inspire Everyone to Take Action.* Penguin.

- Woodward. C. (2005). *Winning!* Hodders Paperbacks.

ACKNOWLEDGEMENTS

To my lovely wife, Amanda Presland. Thank you for everything.

To the two gents who mentor and coach me, Chris Hughes and Andrew Priestley. You have both given so much time, energy and advice to help me craft this book; a massive thank you. Your input enabled me to make this subject more engaging; and you both constantly challenge and inspire my approach and thinking.

Thank you to those who took the time and effort to read and comment on earlier copies of the manuscript: Dan Carlton, Marie Kershaw, Richelle Sparks, Debbie Sinclair and Rachel Standford.

Thank you also to those who gave their time to read the final version of the book and provide testimonials.

Thank you to everyone associated with the *ParentaTrust* who are committed to making a difference in developing nations.

And lastly, but most importantly, thank you to all *Parenta* staff who work so tirelessly and with so much passion to make our thriving company what it is today.

ABOUT THE AUTHOR

Allan Presland is the founder and CEO of Parenta, the UK's largest provider of business support systems to the *Early Years* sector.

Parenta works with over 5,000 childcare providers of various sizes worldwide. He has personally visited over 1,000 childcare settings over the last 17 years.

He has vast experience of witnessing exemplary childcare provision as well as those who need to change. His experience has been translated into this book to provide a guide for those who want to transform their businesses.

Allan is also the Chairman and CEO of *Lara Group PLC,* a listed public company which owns Parenta as well as many other education companies.

Lara brings together quality childcare provision, as well as childcare support services. *Lara* aims to become a major player within the global education sector.

Allan is also the founder of the *ParentaTrust,* a charity that provides pre-school education to orphaned and disadvantaged children in East Africa.

The *ParentaTrust* aims to build ten pre-schools and arrange sponsorship for 1,500 children under five, within the next ten years.

Contact

Website	www.Parenta.com
Resources	www.*Parenta.com/resources*
Blog	www.*allanpresland.com*
Email	
Allan Presland	*allan@Parenta.com*
ParentaTrust	*info@ParentaTrust.org*
Twitter	*@AlPres*

9 780995 605145